WHERE'S HOME?

BOBBI RATHERT

WHERE'S HOME?

PEOPLE EXPERIENCING HOMELESSNESS IN LA CROSSE COUNTY SHARE THEIR STORIES ON A QUEST FOR UNDERSTANDING, BELONGING, AND STABILITY

Hey There, Hannah

CONTENTS

CONTENTS

DISCLAIMER

---

*The stories in this book reflect each participant's reminiscence of experience.
Some names, locations, and identifying characteristics may have been altered
at the participants' request to protect the privacy of persons, places, and events depicted.*

*Stories told are for informational and experiential purposes only, to convey experiences
and perceptions of the subject. No harm is intended to any named
or perceived person, place, business, or procedure.*

*Dialogue for each participant was obtained through face-to-face interviews about the
participants' real-life experiences and recorded in real-time via a talk-to-type application.
Some details may have been altered during the auto-type transfer and the editing process,
but factual information has been maintained to the best of the ability of the technology and
means used.*

DEDICATION

In tribute to anyone who has lost
family, friends, health, and opportunity,
their inner peace and dignity,
a sense of security and self,
the comfort of home,
or their very life,
because of homelessness.

A CHANGE OF HEART

BOBBI RATHERT and the story that led to the creation of this book.

I was sixteen and still growing up in Iowa when my parents urged me to apply for a summer position in Chicago. It was 1971 and I wasn't looking for a live-in job, but I was hired anyway. My family drove me to La Crosse and put me on an eastbound passenger train.

I remained onboard until we pulled into Union Station on Canal Street where I met a young doctor who handed me an infant. I followed him out of the train station and his five other little ones trailed behind. They were in my care for the next two summers as I fell in love with the city.

My Iowa town had a census of about 3600 people and one stoplight. Today the population is almost the same but now there are two stoplights. My upbringing was simple so I wasn't very worldly but plenty naïve. Yet only one step outside the Amtrak station, I was smitten with the big urban life surrounding me. I loved the massive number of people and the energy of the continuous commotion.

As an adult, I rode the Jackson Park line to work every day and got off at the Harrison stop south of Jackson. Across from the subway exit, unhomed people came out of Pacific Garden Mission carrying all their belongings to spend the day on the streets. I loved Chicago and everything in it, including these people about whom I knew nothing.

I walked from the subway to my job on Wabash just past an old Greek restaurant where a brick-and-mortar garden box sat at each side of its door. Some people who left the Mission sat on the cement edges asking for money and smoking cigarettes. I became accustomed to them there so we nodded to each other as if we were friends or neighbors.

One morning, the ledges were vacant. As I approached, I saw that the restaurant owner had poured a thick stripe of wet cement along the flower box edges. He then stuck shards of broken bottle glass pointed upward in the concrete. That was the end of resting on the flower boxes. I can't say any more about that. I didn't understand it then. I don't understand it now.

Outside the Chicago post office, an old bent woman stood most days. I didn't know her name, but I called her Lena to myself. During those years, I went about my business and didn't engage with Lena until I decided to take her some groceries. When I pulled to the curb and spoke to her, she told me to meet her at an SRO two blocks east and around the northwest corner.

I did and she arrived just after. I loaded up with sacks and followed her up the flights of dark stairs and down a creaking unlit hall. Doors opened as people peered out when we passed slowly. It was a corner room near the end where Lena unlocked the door and motioned. The room was tiny but filled with ceiling-high heaps of sacks packed with groceries. I didn't understand it. We neither spoke and I left my bags upon the others.

I never named this group of people, not homeless or vagrant, nor bums or transients. Nothing. They were part of my city life left unexplained and ignored. They lived in everyone's periphery, including mine.

After thirty years, I finished my work in Chicago and moved to southwest Wisconsin. Even though it wasn't exactly my home county, I assumed things would return to the familiar small-town life of before, fair and slow, after my life of work. But I worried it would be too homogenous and I'd grow to dread it.

I had purchased a ridgetop farm southeast of La Crosse but came to town for provisions. I saw people who lived on the streets here, too, *'just like Chicago,'* I thought to myself. I didn't remember this from growing up in the region. So these people living outside stayed on the edge of my mind and I remained complacent. Like Chicago. On a deep level, it was bothersome and I didn't like the way I felt. I didn't understand it. So I overlooked it like a blurred background.

I finally moved to La Crosse for a full-blown retirement where my complacency continued. I presumed no one was doing much to help the homeless community and surely I didn't know what to do. I did not try very hard and kept them on the fringe.

Ultimately, for reasons explained on the back cover of this book, I made a plan to interview the people who were homeless in La Crosse. I went to Tent City and the spaces on the street and in parks where I had seen them with their things. I was surprised by the potency of my feelings when I realized I had no idea what I was doing. I didn't belong, that was obvious. I had no knowledge or education about this, no training at all. *'Why am I doing this?'* I repeatedly thought. I regretted my idea and felt stuck in a singular thought about unhomed people. I couldn't get them to fit nicely into my usual empathy and compassion for others.

In Chicago, the unhoused people smelled on the buses, were dirty and disheveled, and always wanted something. I let this be enough. I didn't know who they were or why they were everywhere but, maybe, I didn't want to know. None of it made sense to me anyway. It seemed like a lot of work to figure it out and who knew where to begin. I certainly didn't. And I couldn't get clear why it made me angry.

I went ahead with my idea to interview people in the parks, and the tent encampment on the north bank of the river across from Friendship Gardens. It was an idea. But with no amount of plan.

When I started to hear stories, I felt clumsy. A voice in my mind kept asking me, *'What are you doing!?'* I was so embarrassed of myself that I was even out there and obviously over my head. I didn't understand any part of it and felt awkward and ill-prepared. But then, I wondered, *'How does a person get prepared for this anyway?'*

I asked questions that were too simple and had no depth, but my deep ones made me roll my eyes at myself. *'What are some of your dreams or goals?'* I asked and then privately shook my head. *'Oh my gosh, dreams and goals! Are you kidding me?'* I just couldn't get it right.

I wanted to quit and forget I ever thought to do this. I hadn't understood this group of people or the reasons for their circumstances over my entire life, so why start now? I began to justify quitting. I felt frustrated and inexperienced. When I made secret plans to end the project, the voice in my head reminded me, *'You opened your big mouth and started something. You can't just back out now!'* So I kept going, dragging myself out there, procrastinating, and on some days, having the dreads. But then, something changed.

The people started expanding, no longer in my periphery like paper dolls. They began to take shape and dimension. I began to remember names and their deepening stories. I could recognize faces and distinguish them from one another. I was receiving phone calls asking if I was coming out, or informing me that their friends wanted to speak with me. And their voices, I could recognize them, too! And most of all, I started to feel compassion. I cared about them and even liked some of them.

I shared nothing about myself and was never asked. The project was not about me, it was clear, and somehow, we all knew it. Their lives were the focus, maybe for the first time ever, and no one was ever short on sharing.

It's almost five months now that I've listened to stories, feelings, and, yes, some dreams and goals. I've supplied food, cigarettes, medicine, some camp gear, and a request for Velcro. Yet, all those things have seemed incidental and, sometimes, unnecessary. We have a relationship now. People. Not paper dolls. With much deeper needs than just objects and provisions.

As the stories poured out, the flat people filled with personalities and histories, some sorrows and strengths, memories of moms, brothers, and school, obvious faith and ideas, jobs, hopes, and memories of grandparents, their children, and desires for home. I heard stories of military service, some regrets, health challenges, neglect, and fishing with fathers. Getting cold and yearning for things, like a bath or a night in a bed. Sometimes they are afraid but still have courage. Most of them are loyal and devoted friends. They make do without cars, money, electricity, natural gas, homes, plans, or our respect.

I began to see them and then started to like them. I noticed I was beginning to care about some, but not as much for others, just like any people. Compassion welled in me which was probably dormant for years, from the beginning.

I didn't need to wonder why I was doing this project anymore. The feeling that rose was good and right and matched what was true. These are real people with real stories that used to frighten me. Stories that might keep us complacent, angry, or with a constant lack of understanding.

The word homeless, and the phrase homeless people, don't occur to me. They're people. Now I can't go back to where I was. It's what I was hoping for with this book, but for you to experience a change of heart, not me. But it is me. I feel different. It's *my* heart that has changed and made the world fuller.

This book did what I hoped it would do. But it did it for me. Now I hope you'll read it so it can do it for you.

THE STORIES

The Stories

- Trish Lisota
- Joseph Abey
- Michael Engrebretson
- Trinj
- Jana Boland-Windbiel, One
- Ryan Marks
- Philip Lavenduskey (Bubba)
- Heather Archer
- Greg
- Lucas DeLorenzo
- Brad and dog Zen
- June Hart
- Marcos Perez
- Jeffrey Brandt
- Jana Boland-Windbiel, Two

TRISH LISOTA

TRISH LISOTA told her story while we sat in the Karuna House living room. "So me and my brother lived in South Carolina. My dad was in the military, so my mom, you know," she trailed off and seemed to be thinking about something. Then she continued, "So he did the best he could."

"We were very structured, very! You know, homework first, then chores, you know, and then we got to run around, basically, because we were latchkey kids, so to speak. We could go swimming anytime we wanted and probably should have been watched a little bit more than we were," she admitted. "But we were, you know, we were responsible."

"Then, our dad went to Bosnia when I was eleven, so I went to Colorado to visit my mom." I interrupted Trish, "When would this have been, what year?" She said, "When I was eleven, so I was born in 1981, so it was 1992-ish, yeah. When my dad was overseas, after his fiancé left him, he met another woman who helped to raise us a little bit."

But while in Colorado, I decided to move in with my mom because I was missing that female part, and I think a little bit of my dad has resentment towards me a little bit because, after that, he got married. My brother stayed with him and I stayed in Colorado for twenty-two years. I had both my kids there."

"As a single mom, I went to school at Pikes Peak Community College. My degree is in interior design," Trish explained. "I worked at a major furniture store within six months and then was promoted to lead designer."

"I raised my kids until they were eight and six. By then, everybody had moved away from Colorado, so I decided..." she said, "Well, you know, being raised in the military, we bounced around all the time. We were from North Carolina, South Carolina, and bopping all over. Mostly, we ended up in South Carolina. But then, like I said, I wanted more stability when I moved with my mom. When she left, she moved to Missouri so I decided to follow her there."

"Then I got engaged," she continued, "but that didn't work out. So, you know, with my kids, I wanted to come up here because my dad always begged me to come here. He'd say, *'You know you were meant to be with us. You're meant to be with us!'* So I thought that's where I was supposed to be. Nobody's going to raise my son to be a man better than my grandpa, my brother, and my dad."

"So, we're all up here. What happened was, I moved up here. My dad came to get me and my kids and we moved here. Within a matter of two years, I was drinking a half gallon of alcohol a day!" I asked, "Do you know why you suddenly began drinking that much?" Trish explained, "Alcohol runs in our family. It's very normalized. I didn't realize at the time what was happening because it was so normalized. But I was depressed so I was drinking."

"I didn't want to get hungover so I would start drinking in the mornings. The science part of it, the chemical in my brain, changed so fast that I had seizures if I didn't drink. Just that quickly, that quickly, within a matter of two years. I remember, wow, yes, I was having my brother and my dad take my kids because I was sloppy drunk! I would be passed out by the time they came home. I knew that I needed help."

"My dad tried to get me some help. We contacted Jackson County and I got into treatment. Jackson County paid for me to be in treatment. I went to treatment for six months, then when I got out, I relapsed. I had pancreatitis, lost forty-five pounds in ten days, and had to be carried out of my house. It was so bad that I almost died," Trish said. "Because I blew a .49, the doctor said, *'For you to blow a forty-nine, you actually could have died. Remember, most people would be dead! Your blood alcohol was almost fifty percent.'* He was very alarmed."

"We have alcoholics in our family so I've always had a tolerance for it, even when I was younger. I partied here and there, and nobody could tell that I was drunk. I could handle it, yeah. It was my dad, he's a drinker. He's a beer drinker and always had his bouts throughout his life, you know. He's been drinking whiskey, and too much of that, so he's learned that he has to lay off the hard stuff and just stick to beer."

"I don't want to get whiskey. I was just going to drink beer. But, at the time, I was in the hospital and realized that my dad had already raised his kids. My brother and his wife live up here, too. I wanted my son to learn to be a man, and my brother and his wife had just found out they couldn't have children. I called my brother and said, *'Please, take my kids. They're eight and six. Dad already raised his kids.'*

"My brother said, *'If we're going to do it, we're going to do it legally.'* So I did the temporary guardianship and, at the time, I didn't know we should have discussed it more. I think, looking back, we should have had better communication. They kept them from me, completely!" I asked Trish for clarification, *"Are you saying that you lost your children completely, without knowing you wouldn't have access to them?"* She said, "Well, it wasn't a temporary guardianship. I couldn't touch it for two years. I tried to go back and get visitation for once a month."

"I was in treatment, and had been following treatment, you know, and ended up in a situation similar to drug court for two and a half years. It was my longest bout of sobriety - a year and twelve days," Trish said. "And in that year and twelve days, I saw my children maybe one time! That's because my brother and his wife didn't know. There's no manual for it and they're thinking, *'This is not healthy.'* Time goes by and my kids are thriving so they don't want that negativity in their life. I get that! It shouldn't have been that way though," she lamented. "That's my thought anyway."

"They had a lawyer," Trish explained. When I asked her if she had a lawyer also, she said, "No, because I didn't think that I needed one. I didn't think it was necessary. I went to treatment, got two jobs, and got a three-bedroom apartment expecting to get my kids back! But they said no! At the same time, looking back though, it only took two years for me to get to that half a gallon a day," Trish reasoned. "All they knew was what they saw. I was here for those two years, yeah but, for all they knew, my kids had been dealing with it for eight and six years. You see what I'm saying?" she asked.

"I didn't communicate that with my brother. So they took these kids. I'd been through hell probably, you know, so they're going to keep them from me." Then I asked about her dad, "Was your dad involved with your brother at this time?" Trish answered, "Yeah, he was. I mean, the thing is that we are very proud people. Proud, you know. I think they just expected me to be able to tell my brother. But I didn't tell him! I never showed up on the doorstep and said, *'Hey, I've been clean for a year! Let me see my kids!'* Trish admitted. I asked her, "Do you know why you didn't do that?" Trish replied with one word. "Shame," she said.

Explaining some of her process, Trish continued, "I've had a lot of therapy, okay. Because, being in a drug court setting, they made me see a therapist. If I didn't see my therapist, they would send me to jail! I love that program, by the way, it's a just program, really it is," she said. "I was in it for two and a half years when they said, *'We have to let you go. You're not going to graduate. You're just treading water,'* and I know that I was doing that, for my own safety, you know. I was just doing enough to keep me safe, but not enough to, you know..." Trish trailed off.

Continuing to describe her experience, Trish admitted, "I had resources, but not enough to really like doing it on my own. So they told me, *'We have to let you go. The program is a yearlong but you've been at it for two years.'* I was hanging on, right? But part of it was the therapy."

"I saw my therapist for eight years! She just recently, I think last year, she retired. I haven't gotten a new one yet. It was hard for me to see her, you know, to just be able to trust her with my story. Through the ins and outs of it, I learned to trust her and tell her everything. I learned that my biggest thing is keeping up with my mental health because using and my addiction, all that is only a symptom of my mental health. Everything falls along with all these consequences that follow for years later. That's a path of a lifetime," Trish described.

"My son is twenty-one. He just had a little girl in October with his girlfriend." She nodded and smiled when I said, "You're a grandmother!" She added, "My daughter still lives with my brother and his wife. She will be eighteen." Then I asked, "So they kept them and raised them well for you?" Trish answered, "Yep." "Have you seen them?" I asked. "I've seen them on and off," Trish said, "We are working on our relationship. But the thing is, they were young when they kept them from me. When they got older, they said, *'It's up to the kids.'* But at that point, they didn't know me anymore. I get that, so I have to accept my part." I asked Trish to talk about her part of being separated from her children.

Trish gave it some thought and then said, "The total part is not on my shoulders. I very much know that there are a lot of pieces. I'm just trying to see different perspectives, you know, and understand it. I'm pretty self-aware, I think," she said as she seemed deep in thought. "Tell me," I said, "Do your children want to get to know you?" Trish answered, "I think so. I think they're scared." "Are you thinking that they are afraid of you?" I asked, "Is that how you see it? Or afraid of what might happen?" She answered, "I don't think they know everything behind it. So it's kind of like my family up here. It's kind of like, *'out of sight, out of mind'* unfortunately. It sucks," she said.

Switching topics, Trish said, "As far as the homelessness part goes, the treatment helped me. There's a little bit of transitional housing for women. It's sober living, not much though for the women's part. In this area, there is a lot of housing for men, but not the same for women. That is something I really would like to eventually get into. I'm so glad to see Karuna House. Like the Ruth house, which was hit or miss," she said. "You could smoke pot one time after you've been addicted for ten years, then you're out! That's not how it should be! I always said there should be a middle ground, you know. If you smoke pot, you're going to get kicked out of Karuna House? I doubt it! This is the middle ground! This is perfect!" Trish declared. "My uncle lives here at Karuna, and one of my best friends, Bubba."

"It is my Uncle Mike. He's in a room across from Bubba. He's not from around here but came here because of me," Trish said. "I told him the resources were here. He finds them better than I do, unfortunately. The shelters and stuff are full, and I've been kicked out for being fifteen minutes late!" When I asked Trish, "Where are you staying now, or are you struggling with that? Are you living in the marsh?" "No, I don't even have a tent," she said. "Where do you sleep then, if you have no place or even a tent in Tent City?" I asked. "The other day, I slept by the train station. I just try to find places to go," Trish said quietly. I asked, "If you had a tent, what would you do?" After a moment of reflection, Trish answered, "I'd probably go down by the marsh and sleep. I'd go down by five other homeless people." I wondered if Trish had a sleeping bag but she answered, "No," when I asked. "I don't even have blankets or a sleeping bag."

I remembered a spare sleeping bag and matte that I had in storage at home so I said, "I can get you a tent, and I have a sleeping bag and matte that you can have if you want it." Trish said, "Thank you, okay, I appreciate that. I'll find the homeless community and I'll just go be by them. That's what I did before. I lived down at Tent City before they shut it down. Several years back, there was the same place, you know, and the problem was that they didn't clean up after themselves," she explained and then added, "I'm one of the ones that try to show respect because...they're the ones that give us a bad name."

Trish continued to express her disappointment that there wasn't housing available to her. "This is why we need Karuna House, but they're getting those people off the street. But me, I'm still floating around, right? I'm not getting this, a place like Karuna House. I'm not, because I'm not a nuisance, which is terrible! I've been on and off this list, the housing list, you know, where people get housing. They get their rent paid indefinitely! Where am I on that list? I would be in transitional living. I'm not an emergency. I'm not actually on the street like they are, so they need more. They need more than me. I get that, but what about me!?" Trish puzzled.

"The ones that fall through the cracks, like the ones that...you know what I mean?" Trish tells about when she struggled to abide by rules while housed. "This past winter I was sheltered but I've gotten kicked out a couple of times. You know, rules and everything. Because I had drugs, I get it, you know. I did it once and got seven days, okay. Trish imitated what she was told at the shelter, *'She didn't learn her lesson now, okay, now try two weeks!'* She continued to speak like those who oversee the rules. *'This time fifteen minutes because you did it one time and we said we let you slide. Now you did it twice, now you get kicked out for a week!'* Trish continued to describe her frustration with balancing her addiction and the need for shelter.

"It is a good program," she admits. So I asked her, "Do you want to continue to be at the Salvation Army?" Trish is adamant, "No! I want to have my own place, yeah!" I questioned her, "Right now, what is your option to living in a tent?" Trish thought a minute and then answered, "It's warm enough, so I think if I had a sleeping bag, I would rather, you know, do that right now."

I asked, "Do you have a social worker or somebody who works with you to guide you about getting into housing?" Trish said, "I just called him today and I have an appointment tomorrow at eleven o'clock. I'm hoping I'm on the verge of getting something."

I told Trish, "Don't give up on it. Today you'll get your tent." And she added, "I'm sober today, too." I tried to explore her experience with sobriety, "Well, how do you feel being sober? Can you talk about what it is like to live in the cycle of sobriety and using? How far are you able to go with sobriety? I'm wondering if you are sober because you don't have money or because you're trying to stay sober?" Trish was expressionless. "Because I don't have money," she said. I replied, "It sounds like money stands between you and using and between you and sobriety"

Continuing the subject of her addiction, Trish said, "I was on the methadone program. I just got off of it. It's almost going on two weeks now. But here I go, if I had money, I'd go running around, okay? Like today, I've been hanging out all day. I could go and try to find money. It's very easy for a woman, as you probably know, to find money. To go get it, right? So I'm trying but it's all on me. That's what I mean, that is what's happening." I asked, "Would you say that you're not getting the help you need, or the stability or shelter? That it's all on your shoulders? You aren't getting the medication or nutrition so that you can focus on getting clean? Can you talk more about that?"

Trish gave this a moment of thought and then said, "I would say it's impossible, yeah, because a person needs stability to do that. I need a routine. I need someone to watch over me. I know that I can do it but, right now, I can't," she explained. "How long has it been since you took that first drink?" I asked her. Trish said, "Ohh, the drink that switched...by the way, I switched from alcohol to meth and heroin. I did that how soon after?" she thought aloud. "I first tried meth in 2016, all right? I would say 2012, okay, February of 2012 for alcohol. And then, four years passed when I discovered methamphetamine. I realized that I was ADHD which was a lot of the reason why I

self-medicated."

Trish continued, "They started putting me on Vyvanse *(Vyvanse is lisdexamfetamine, a prescription medication that treats ADHA and binge eating disorder)*. That's when I was on Vyvanse for over a year. I wouldn't drink! So I went, *'Oh my God! that's my solution!'* I didn't need to use substances! I don't use alcohol or drugs when I use this medication. I do use alcohol and drugs, all funked up, and falling over, but I do it to maintain and be able to function. I've heard that before, with ADHD, you get Adderall, so amphetamine, right?" Trish further explained that, in the past, she had a prescription for Vyvanse in a nearby county. But when she lost her shelter there and could find nothing to rent, she had to move to La Crosse. However, she was unable to attain the medication in her new location.

Unraveling the complications of ADHD and prescription medication is a multiple-layered problem for a person without stable resources. Self-medicating on the streets, finding and keeping shelter and necessary supports, and generally finding the path to a healthier, more functional life sound impossible for Trish and others who are living outside or in uncertain housing. I asked Trish how old she was. "I'm forty-two," she answered.

"Can you think about a future for yourself, maybe when you're fifty years old?" I asked. "How do you want life to look for you by then?" Without any hesitation, Trish said, "I want to be helping people who, like me, are falling through the cracks. People don't see," she said. "I used to be able to get through the day just by watching out for the old people who drank at the park. They'd lay on their beds, and I would give them a beer. I'd steal bottles for them. I knew how it felt, you know? I didn't have to feel that way anymore, but I didn't want them to feel that way. That's how I lived for three and a half years."

"I didn't even realize I was on the street for three and a half years when I was put in jail. Then I was placed at the Ophelia House *(note: Ophelia House is a collaboration between the La Crosse YMCA, Justice Support Services, and the Department of Justice that offers gender-specific programming designed to provide full services for women in the program.)* I was finally able to live like a human being again. They helped me with Drug Court because one of my charges was for an empty baggie. They are good people. Most services don't do Drug Court until many felonies later. But I did it right away because I knew I needed the help."

"My grandpa is a retired captain of the Sheriff's Department here, by the way. So I know those officers. They came up to me and said, *'Trish, is there anything we need to know? Anything you know that you want to tell us? How is the park at night?'* I'd say that it's pretty sad. Then the officers would ask, *'Is there anything we should know?'* I'd answer that they should go check this or that person who was in the parking ramp."

"That was four years before they put all the playgrounds up so everybody was living in the parking ramps. There even were microwaves in the parking ramps. But this old man was not doing well. I gave him clothes to change. He would tip over so that's why I asked the officer to check on him. They took him to the hospital where he died. He was that bad! In that whole place, I knew he needed to be checked on," Trish said as a way to explain how she wants to care for others who are experiencing street life and addiction as she has.

She continued to tell more of her story by sharing some of the challenges she has encountered. "That's the whole family pride thing. I didn't want to give my grandpa a bad name. I knew that they stuck me with an empty baggie and made me sit for forty-eight days on my first charge. No signature bond, no reduction of bond. Two weeks later, they made me stay there until they figured something out. I know they did that on purpose. Don't you think it sounds like I'm just not getting breaks or help? I am smart enough to know. I'm not on disability. I'm not trying to suck up all the resources. I can work, you know, I can!" Trish affirmed.

I asked Trish when she last had work. "I was working when I was at the Salvation Army. But there was a girl there with a personality conflict. I struggled with that a lot, but I can work. I was working at group homes in Viroqua for a little while." I continued to ask more about work, "Do you want to work now, or do you feel you need some support first so you can get better?" Trish answered, "I want support so I can be better! That's what I want so I can reach out and do the kind of work that I want to do!"

I shared with her what I had heard from unsheltered people in the community. "People with stories similar to yours have this cyclical experience of start-stop-start-stop. They can briefly stop using alcohol and drugs, or find housing and work. But it doesn't last, as they continue in a sequence of going forward, and then falling back. Do you feel it is because people have such needs and are not getting the full amount of help they need to stop cycling?" I asked Trish. "Right!" she answered, "It's not going to happen like that to start a new life."

"People are going from a park bench to under the bridge to the park to the tent! I am from this town. I was born here even though I was raised in South Carolina and lived twenty-two years in Colorado. I feel connected with this place like it's a vortex."

"Anybody would say, *'Okay, if you're going to be homeless, at least go somewhere warmer!'* I walked around wearing a snowsuit for three and a half years! I'd bebop all over! But I have been housed between here and there. I don't want to be on the street anymore! I know what it's like! I've been through it! I don't want to do that again! I don't want to be down in the city again."

"People say that the homeless people don't want to be housed. A lot of these people don't want to be housed, yes, but there are a lot who do. A lot of them have their rent paid indefinitely. All they have to do is follow the rules, okay? They can go through three different apartments, using up resources three different times before they get kicked out of the program."

"I used to tell my uncle when he got his apartment, I'd say, *'Mike, you don't understand these people are not going to be there for you when you lose this place. You don't understand what you have here. You have an apartment, Mike!'* Trish said."

"My uncle has a good heart. Everybody wants to help each other. But not all of them, no, because some of them are only out for themselves, unfortunately. Out of desperation, they've given up, right? Well, look at what we're ending up with - the cycle! It is a cycle. It's a cycle and nobody knows how to stop it! Or they don't want to stop it because it's too complicated, right? Some people just don't know how to live."

Changing the subject to speak of a friend who recently became housed, Trish started talking about Bubba, "I can't imagine what Bubba feels after thirty-four years out. You have to learn how to be a human again, right? The bathroom, the shower, and a routine. If I don't clean up, these people are going to be mad at me! Like the girls who were yelling at me in jail. I told them, *'Listen, you don't understand. I've been on the street! I don't have to clean the toilets so, if I need to do it, just tell me!'* Communication is huge! People don't talk, you know."

"I don't think people of any kind of empowerment or money understand what I'm describing. What they think is, *'We have a garage apartment upstairs and we'll give it to you. Then you should get better now, right?'* But that's not what happens. It's not that easy! It's not, no, no!" Trish exclaimed. "I just want a place with no roommates because I've had roommate situations where it was going to work. Then they're the ones who become in charge so it just never works out, you know."

"For your dream to be realized by fifty years old and work on this cycle, get a job, and housing, do you talk to your social worker about it so you can get help with your goal?" I asked. "But you need the supportive help that is necessary. Only you can say what that is and ask for what you need as resources. You can tackle these challenges with assistance." I reminded her.

Trish said, "Yes, that's true. There is a lot out there, a lot of help here in this town. But unfortunately, some of those people are just like I said, they're just going through it, you know. They're going to the department and that's wasted money that could have been available to somebody like me. I'm not saying I'm better than them, but I do want something better in my life. I want that!"

Mentioning her friend Bubba again, Trish said, "I used to know exactly where to find Bubba in the parking ramp. That was his spot, you know. It's so nice to see him in a place like this, at the Karuna House. Now he needs to learn how to live like a human, too, because you should see his bedroom!" She smiled and glanced toward Bubba across the room. I laughed and added, "I've heard! I've heard the tales about the condition of his room!" Trish said, "It's not how he was socialized. I understand. He just doesn't say, *'Okay, I'm going to get up and clean my room today.'* That's not what we do. We have to work at surviving! We need an advocate, yes!"

"It can happen because there's a lot of help in this town and you desire it. As you age, it will become more difficult to be living unsheltered," I said to Trish. She thought and then said, "At some point, it's either do or die, yeah. But we need things like these transitional housing situations."

"When I was in treatment," she continued, "I went from the three-month transitional housing, back and forth, because they didn't know where else to put me. I didn't have anything else. Something was going on behind the scenes that I didn't necessarily know about either," she said. "I just found that out this week. You know, a meth addiction is like the devil's got your foot. But if I was on Vyvanse, I wouldn't need meth. I don't want to be high. I just want to feel okay. Vyvanse is just like Adderall but it's less addictive. But they won't give it to me here in La Crosse."

"If I had a place, I would transport to go see the man in Richland Center where I received Vyvanse medically. I know I can do anything I want, yes, and that I can put my mind to do. Whatever it is I want, but there are obstacles and life happens. I just don't know how to deal with that all the time," Trish explained. I replied, "If I didn't know you had an appointment tomorrow, I would suggest the first thing you do is get an appointment with a social worker. But you already did and you have that appointment already! You can use that to your advantage as you set up a plan with your goal in mind."

Trish appeared to think about plans to get her needs met. "If I can get a ride to the methadone clinic in the morning if I want to see the doctor again..." she thought aloud. "I'm already off methamphetamines, but I was on methadone for the last couple of months. I started using heroin when my two best friends died a week apart last May. It was then that I started doing heroin. I don't know why. It's like a self-sabotage thing or something. I just got really sad."

"Then my friend said, *'Just go get methadone. At least that way you're not sick and you can function. You can choose to get high if you want. You can up your dose,'* she said, *'You go every day to try to chase after drugs so why don't you just get that out of the way?'* Okay, true, my medical pays for my ride there," Trish said as she was seemingly concocting a plan. "I know I don't want to be kicked out of places, living in doorways, dying out here. I could have a whole new life at forty-two."

We talked about how I could get a tent, sleeping bag, and matte to her. Trish suggested, "You could bring it here to Karuna and give it to my uncle. He's here. I'll go find the homeless community, at least for now. I'm in constant contact with people I know who have places out there. I'd rather be by the homeless community," Trish said, "At least we watch out for each other, you know."

"Why isn't there a Driftless House for women?" Trish asked. "There's one that has eighteen beds for men, but not one that has even five beds for women. It's needed, yeah, it needs to be available. But you can only stay there for a week, I think. What is that, you know, in a week you can't do anything, right? In a week, you're supposed to snap out of it? I want to be right, all right, so that would be cool to carry this out and be seen in this town in a different light. Not to have it be the way it is would be nice. To have an apartment or a home, I do want my own home. I'd even take one of those tiny little homes.

Those tiny homes, you know, like Denver has - the tiny home villages, I think. That would be cool to get that here. I don't need a big house. It's just me, you know."

Trish reminded me, "It's been twelve years. That's a long time. My family doesn't know what's been going on in between. I can't just say, okay, *'same story - different day.'* I am supposed to do something, but I'm shameful and guilty, you know. I don't want to live with my dad for the rest of my life. I want my own place. I want to earn for myself next time."

As we closed our afternoon discussion, Trish and I spoke about how she could return to her dad and family. However, she agreed that she must first get assistance for herself by reaching for help and continuing to move forward with social service support. Thank you, Trish, for sharing your stories and desires about the future.

WHERE'S HOME?

JOSEPH ABEY

JOSEPH ABEY spoke with me in early April at the main library. He began by stating that he was born in Wyoming. "Buffalo, Wyoming," he said proudly. "In Johnson County." He continued sharing openly, "I will turn forty in October and I was born in 1984. It was the 21st of October, yep, which was a Sunday."

"You even know the day!" I told him. "Yep, because I've done my stuff for so long that I know what day it was when you come back to it enough," Joseph explained, then continued, "Yeah, it's based on every week. It's really hard to have a birthday during Leap Year because you're still young! That's interesting because, if you think about it, Leap Year, those people have a birthday only once in four years. The same for the president, every four years!" he said. "I'm a Libra and Scorpio. The Libra and Scorpio Cusp because my birthday falls on the 21st of October," he said emphatically about its importance. "And the 21st of October is almost a Halloween baby. Yep, so that's why, my birthday sits between both of those." I responded to him, "That is very interesting. Thanks for explaining it."

Joseph was enthusiastic and went on with his story, "So when I was sixteen, I pretty much rebelled against my mom because I wasn't going to hurt a dog. It was the neighbor's dog. She wanted me to shoot it because it came in our yard. It's not right, okay, so she kicked me out at that time. Yep, someone shot the dog because I wouldn't do it." When I asked if he would talk about his family structure, he said, "In my household, I had my sisters. Jesse was another black sheep. She took me off the streets. She's my blood sister who raised me as a kid. The only person I ever knew to go, too, was my sister. She's in Wyoming. Newcastle, Wyoming," Joseph said. "Jessica Lynn Rocco, that's my half-sister."

Joseph continued to speak about his life and his mother. "My mom gave her life to work, but out of that journey, I learned that the streets had become my home when no one else would teach me. After my dad died, I had to carry my mom. It's because of my dad," he said. "My mom was a narcissist. When someone can't control you, and you finally stand up against them, they don't want anything to do with you. They see you as a problem because they can't control you anymore."

"During my whole journey, I've been out on the streets. The people out there have watched over me," Joseph opened up to describe how he has been cared for by others living outside. "They've taken me under their wings and taught me how to survive out here. How to keep warm, how to make it."

I asked Joseph if he had been living unsheltered for the past twenty-five years. He answered, "Yes, but between that, I did get into a place. I had such a caring heart to give people a chance. That caused me to lose my apartment. My dream was actually to be a computer person so I started that course. But then, I lost my apartment. I lost everything because of my choice to be a big-hearted guy. People can stomp on me," he said as he lowered his head. "Because when I asked them to help, *'Can you go out there and pick up your dog's poo or I'm going to lose my place,'* they refused! They just got mad and left me. They picked up all my stuff and sold it! But I'm fine with that," he conceded. "I don't hurt people, because I learned what my dad taught me. He had lots of smarts and taught me *'If it's an item, it can be replaced. But a person can't be replaced,'* my dad instructed me."

After Joseph's Dad died, he said that his mom was angry and wanted to take it out on the neighbor's dog. "All because she lost her soulmate," Joseph reasoned. "My mom became abusive from the beginning. I started getting abused and being hurt. She was my guardian but for all I went through, so much, I brought myself through it. I had to better myself because I realized I started to pick up somebody else's ways and it changed me from being me. So I worked to become a better honest person," Joseph said.

"Being mentally disabled and on the street was not easy at age sixteen. I had to get up when the sun came up, pack up my stuff, and get to school every day. I did it because I wanted to make something of my life. That's why I did it."

"In the middle of my journey," Joseph continued, "I was homeless from sixteen until twenty. I learned how to survive on the streets. While growing up there, I found there were elements that no one knew how to deal with, you know. None of the people, none of them, would know how to do it because Wilmington, Wyoming is mountainous. There are mountains there and, growing up in the mountains, I learned how to respect nature and the people. Because if you can't respect nature, it isn't going to respect you!"

Joseph described growing up in nature and that it has helped him connect with it to find peace. He shared a story about a turtle that he pulled in a wagon. "I fell in love with that turtle and named it Michelangelo, like the Ninja turtle," he said. But after an altercation, someone killed it. Joseph could tell that it was an older snapping turtle because of its spots. When I asked him how he learned this, Joseph explained, "I was an A and B student in school and I liked Biology. I was on meds but my dad said I didn't need them. I could work with him to get the knowledge, but it would be the hard way. I've learned everything the hard way. Out of my hard life, I became smarter," Joseph said.

Continuing to describe how he has struggled with depression and been suicidal, he said, "I was born with it, being mentally disabled. Every mental health professional out there has said I read like a table of contents, like a textbook. I've overcome a lot but the two I still have are severe ADHD and autism. I am among other autistic people. They are geniuses - Aberdeen and Einstein were autistic."

When I asked if he had gotten any significant help with his diagnosis, Joseph said, "I learned I'd have to push forth. Just push forth, push forth, yep, push forth. Be grateful for everything I'm given because you never know when you could lose it," he said.

I switched to the subject of shelter when I asked Joseph, "Where are you staying now?" He explained, "Still home at the Salvation Army, yeah." I asked, "So, you have a place to sleep?" When he answered yes, I asked, "How long does this situation last for you?" Joseph answered, "I'm hoping to get into a place. That's my goal, yep. But it's scary," he said. I asked him, "Is it particularly scary now partly because you're getting older?" He replied, "Yes, I'm turning forty this year. I don't see age as a bad thing. Age is just another day of wisdom you've learned. There's something new each day. Always something new."

Joseph continued but changed the subject. "I have to look after myself before it leads to something dangerous. I am going to protect what I was raised with. I didn't know the true meaning of family and devotion. But it's here on the streets." So I said to him, "I've also heard that from other people who feel loyalty to each other, but they've said that they can get hurt by each other, too." Joseph said, "Yes, right. If you don't have the boundaries to know which one needs to stop right there. It is only created by conflict. Conflict is friction."

"People get themselves worked up. But it doesn't fall on the other person exactly when one could do WWJD – what would Jesus do," Joseph said. I asked him, "What would Jesus do?" He responded, "He turned his right cheek and walked away the bigger man. My dad said, *'The better man who knows right from wrong always walks away and turns the right cheek.'* Joseph said. I asked, "Your dad told you that? How old was your dad when he died?" Joseph answered, "I was sixteen." I asked Joseph if he could talk about his dad's death and what happened to him.

"He was crushed by casing pipes when I was sixteen," Joseph explained further that his father worked in the Wyoming mines where he was killed. He clarified that his father "died when I was fifteen and, at his funeral, I had turned sixteen." "I'm so sorry," I said as he continued, "Mom depended on me for a whole year. I've been through so much. I've seen so many deaths and lost friends on the street. I've lost friends to war. I've lost too much. But everything comes with a price. Nothing is free, it's true. When you lose one, you gain another or you gain knowledge. I am always gaining something new in life." Joseph began to talk about his birthday in October of this year and that he will be forty years old.

To bring our interview to a close, I asked Joseph to talk about what he imagines his life looking like when he becomes fifty years old. I said, "Between now and then, how would you like to be sheltered? Would you want a place like Bubba has, at Karuna House, that you can call your own? Where you would have the right to come and go, not facing danger every day or solving everything on your own?" Joseph's eyes brightened as he smiled, "I could just come out anytime! I want that."

"The thing I want, and that you don't know about, is to not worry about my stuff being stolen. I was raised on this rule called the Golden Rule. *'Do to others as you would have done unto you.'* It is a good foundation rule and it's simple. My dad was homeless for a while, too. He was Wayne William Franks, Robert Frank's brother. My Uncle Robert was his older brother. He's the last boy out of all his brothers but he has a sister, too. She's in a chair because she used to make fireworks and got injured," he said as he relayed more of his family story.

"My bloodline comes from Norway, from Ragnarök." Joseph shared that when his stepfather was with his mom after the death of his dad, there was further abuse in the family. He tells how he and his sister were sexually abused and neglected, and he was disbelieved when he reported his stepfather."

Joseph circles back to his thoughts about the Karuna House. "It is good because there is someone to help with conflicts. You still get to keep your room," he said. I asked him, "So you'd be interested in something like that?" He emphatically replied, "Yes, I would! The streets have done so much for me and my learning. I know how to overcome it because of wisdom. But I don't need to stay on the streets, you're right. But I will stay true to the street. I'm always going to go out and help people on the streets, just as they helped me. But I don't have to stay on the streets," he reasoned. "If I was stronger in my living situation, I'd even be more helpful to the people on the streets!"

To close, I told Joseph, "You are awesome! I thank you so much for sharing with me and being so open with your story."

MICHAEL ENGREBRETSON

MICHAEL ENGREBRETSON and I met in Cameron Park. A friend of his had just collapsed to the ground as we sat down to talk at a nearby table. Another of Michael's friends called 911 and, just as we finished this interview, emergency vehicles arrived at the scene. Despite the near-tragic event unfolding nearby, Michael was calm and seemed to take it as an ordinary experience while expressing no urgency. Others at the park milled about as if nothing was happening near them where another unsheltered person lay unconscious in the grass.

Michael spelled his name for me and answered, "Yep, yep, that's exactly right," when I spelled it back to him.

I asked him to talk about how long he had lived on the streets. "I was on the street a long time ago. What happened is that I kind of got into some trouble as a kid and I ended up in jail. Then I got sent to prison for three and a half years."

I asked, "How old were you when these things happened?" Michael replied, "I was eighteen. When I got out, I had stuff in storage but ended up losing it all. So I had to start from scratch."

"Friends of mine in the past let me stay in their garages or under their porches. They were non-heated and non-air-conditioned, so I had to deal with the heat and the cold. But, you know, at least I had the space heater during winter. At least I got to stay warm and had blankets," he said with relief. "All that was when I lost all my stuff because I couldn't keep up the storage. So I lost it all and had to start over from scratch."

"You were in your twenties by then?" I asked. Michael thought for a minute and then said, "Yeah, just a young guy, yeah. I was living outside for at least a couple of years. But then I was able to get a place with a friend of mine. I looked him up on the north side and, fortunately, I stayed on his porch originally. It was my pastor's porch, but then he let me move in with him since I knew him. I just couldn't bounce around with friends or porch surf anymore," he said.

"I'm forty-nine, and in August, I'll be fifty," Michael said. He agreed that he had been without a permanent home for thirty years of his life. "You've been bouncing around quite a bit. Have you ever had a place for a significant length of time?" I asked. Michael stared into the distance, thinking, and then said, "I stayed with somebody, I think an aunt and uncle of a friend of mine, their aunt and uncle, two years ago. Then I moved into the friend's place on the north side and stayed about six months. After that, I got a place of my own," he said without expression or emotion.

"Now you have a place?" I asked. "It's a lot more years living unhoused than sheltered. How do you feel being inside now?" Michael gave a shallow nod and said, "Good. It's nice to have a roof over my head, yeah. I don't have to leave, no, and nobody takes my stuff. Unfortunately, I did get robbed though, because someone somehow broke into my place. But they didn't get much. They took my safe and mutilated it, but the joke was on them because there was nothing in it. All my valuable stuff is in the safe deposit box I opened in Onalaska."

I asked Michael about having a home of his own now, but still spending his days in the park with the unhoused community. "You stay in your place, and then you come out here and be with your friends. Does it feel like home here at Cameron Park, too?" Michael responded, "Yep. Some of them are homeless. Some are not. I'd say most of them are homeless, but some are not."

"Can you talk about your early years and where you were born and raised?" I asked. "I was born and raised, and lived outside, in La Crosse my entire life. I was born in August at Saint Francis, it's Mayo now. When I was born, we lived on Farnam Street. Then we moved to Tyler and Eighth where we had the house there. Then the landlord sold it. They tore it down and built an apartment building. Then we moved over to Section 8 on Johnson and lived there for most of my life. But at the age of five, my mom and dad got divorced. My mom moved up to Bangor and I lived with my dad from then on. He passed away in 1991, and then I got in trouble."

"I ended up getting locked up. That's where it started, yeah," Michael said and shook his head. "Both my mom and dad passed away. I got a half-sister but she says I should call her my sister. So, yeah, my sister, Tammy lives up in Bangor. I keep in contact with her." I asked Michael if Tammy would help him out if he called. "Yeah, yeah, when she can, yeah. She has some rough spots, too, yeah. She's not doing too well health-wise. She's older, five years older than me," he explained.

"It sounds like you've had a rough time from the very beginning, Michael. It's been challenging for you, hasn't it?" I said. "Yeah, I got into a lot, a *lot* of troubles as a kid, too. You know, being in group homes and foster homes," he trailed off. He talked about being in legal trouble twice in the last dozen years. Once in 2012 as well as in February 2014 when he received the maximum for his charges.

"I made up my mind that I couldn't do this anymore," Michael explained. I just couldn't, and I've been doing good since. That was around 2014, so ten years, yeah," he calculated. When I asked him how long he'd been in his apartment, he answered, "Since December of last year."

"Michael, you have been doing well for about nine and a half years, and now you have had a place for these last six months that you can call home." He smiled, "Yep, and good health kind of, yeah. I've had a stroke already, they said, a silent mini-stroke. That was a couple of years back when I had the flu and pneumonia. My oxygen level went down so it was hard for me to breathe. I had to spend the night at Mayo, yeah. But, oh, and I'm pre-diabetic now. My mama had Type Two diabetes. So I guess it runs in my family, yeah. I have to be careful. I was going to quit smoking and drinking and sugar." Michael said hopefully.

"You appear as if you're doing pretty good. You seem happy," I said. Michael grinned. Then he slowly said, "Yeah, I'm happy, you know. It's good to have a place and not be out in the elements, yeah. I wish everyone could have a place of their own or live with someone. But in this town, this place just doesn't want to do anything," he said as he nodded his head toward downtown. "They just went up north and swept it under the rug, that's right."

I asked Michael, "Is your home situation secure so you don't have to worry about losing it?" He answered, "Well, I got help with it through the county's support. They set me up with it. The housing authority gave me a Section 8 voucher, so I got that. They had a place up for rent over on Division Street, so I applied for it."

"Because of my past criminal record, the executive director denied it. But then he read over the reference letters that I sent with the application, and he reconsidered. I have the furniture I need, almost everything. I'm still looking for a couch," he said. "I have a bed, my towels, and sheets, and two TVs. One in the living room and one in my bedroom." Michael was smiling as he described his home and its comforts. I said, "You are almost fifty and you did it! You have all that you need." He added, "I have a microwave, a stove, and a fridge, too!"

"All of these years, Michael, you haven't had anything but a friend's couch or a porch. But now you have everything you need to live and be safe and comfortable."

Michael was looking satisfied and content, then explained about his employment. "I've had jobs, many different jobs, in my life. Right now, I can't say anything about my work now, because of policies. I don't want to say the wrong thing. If it gets put in your book or something, they can...I don't want any trouble. I can't say where I'm working, but it's a good job. They've cut back on my hours because business is slow right now. But when it starts picking up again, I'll get more hours. I've been working there for a year and eight months."

"That's amazing, Michael, you are taking good care of yourself. These last few weeks, I've interviewed several people who are experienced in living outside. I've gone around and talked to many folks who would like to achieve what you have accomplished. You're life is stabilizing now in comparison to your past and to a some other people's situations out here," I said as we both glanced at the people scattered around Cameron Park that afternoon. "You are an example of the possibility to overcome history and hardship." "Yeah, I know!" he exclaimed. "So just when I get there, you know, it's just getting there, you know. When I get there, stay still!"

Thank you to Michael for sharing his story of restoration, finding work, home, health, security, and happiness.

TRINJ

TRINJ and I met along the riverbank of Tent City on a chilled March day. He wore an oversized jacket without any shirt underneath but did not seem bothered by the low temperature. He told me that he came to the United States from Laos when he was a boy, accompanied by his mother and other family members.

I asked about his life since he arrived in America and now as he's been a resident of our local homeless population. "Being poor, yeah, not much better," he said. "Yeah, I have to survive, but barely surviving."

I asked Trinj if he knew what he would want if change could happen. "What would you like if you could have your life any way you chose?" I said. "I don't know," Trinj said, "Maybe to be like, just be like Superman, to be helpful like Superman, yeah. I won't be Superman and destroy things like you all do in Hollywood movies."

"But I wanted just love and support for me when I came over with my parents." It was apparent that Trinj's life did not improve when he came to America from his war-torn country.

I wondered about his family of origin and whether anyone was still in the local area, so I asked about it. He eagerly explained, "Oh yeah, I had my brother, Chung, and one in Oklahoma, one in Minnesota. Yeah, Minnesota. They're still there, yeah. My brother Lee is the dragon. Now Lee is the oldest."

A friend of Trinj's added that one of them had passed. So Trinj said, "The oldest passed away from struggling with chemicals in Laos. My parents didn't die in Laos, but they're all gone, yeah. My dad passed away in 2000. My mom just died last year, yeah. She had a lot of loss, yeah. It was hard." Trinj's friend urged him further, "Your mother and you are our spiritual healers or readers here in Tent City. What is it, a Shaman?"

He continued asking Trinj how he and his mom went to church as spiritual leaders. "That's still here, no, that was in Laos," Trinj replied. He continued to describe his church attendance, being a Shaman with his mother, and that he has never married or had children. It seemed that Trinj had been alone and without a home for most of his life. He spoke about his relationship with the church, belief in Jesus, the Second Coming, and connection to nature including birds, the heat, and spirituality.

Trinj abruptly ended our conversation by telling me, "I don't want to talk anymore," as he walked away and through the encampment alone. His friend described how Trinj can be seen across the camp doing karate in solitude or meditating by himself, and that he seems unafraid.

Thank you, Trinj, for bearing up and sharing your difficult story.

WHERE'S HOME?

JANA BOLAND-WINDBIEL

JANA BOLAND-WINDBIEL and I sat in the grass under a tree at the public library. Once she overcame initial nervousness, Jana opened up and told her story. "I was born and raised in La Crosse. My family was established here and owned the Myrick Park Zoo where I had a great childhood! I worked, played, and volunteered at the zoo. It was so much fun," Jana said. "So I had a pretty good childhood. But, we were taken from home when I was fourteen years old."

"Our mom was more concerned with her boyfriend and what she was doing at the time. That was only for a couple of years," she explained. I asked, "Was this for your entire teen years? And what about the zoo? Did your mom and dad have the Myrick Park Zoo?"

Jana clarified, "My grandparents had the zoo. My dad died when I was fourteen. I was drinking at the time, and partying a lot, so my dad put me in rehab before he passed away. I was there while he died but, after that, I started the whole drinking, drugs, and getting into all of it at fourteen. Then I got married at sixteen and had my son at seventeen. I haven't seen the father since, so I was a single parent very young."

She continued, "At age twenty, I met Scott number one. That is what I call him and you'll learn why later! He helped me raise my son for the twenty years we were together. He was good and a great provider." Jana explained that, during these years, she went to college to be a paralegal. "Scott and I had a great life and we weren't poor! We were doing good," she said. I asked her, "Had you stopped drinking and doing drugs?" Jana answered, "When I had my son, yes, I did stop. But it was about seventeen years later that Scott started acting violently and a little different. He was starting to have some very odd symptoms. We found out that he had a particular tumor that had grown so large and entangled in his ocular nerve. He was bleeding on his brain, so he had emergency surgery to remove the tumor. They couldn't get it all out, so right now, he's still living with the tumor. He just takes medication for that," Jana said.

"We are no longer together but lost our house due to the medical issues. Scott had a really good job at Great Lakes Cheese but he had to quit it. I was a doctor's technician at Eye Mart Express at that time." Jana agreed when I remarked, "You two were established and rooted in a life together." She elaborated,

"The house was on the north side and was around the area where I grew up. Scott and I were good together until the tumor came. By then I was in my mid-thirties. It was around the year 2011 and my son had graduated high school. That is about when we lost the house, right after that."

Jana explained that she began using meth when her son was twelve. She said, "I don't know how I managed to keep it all together for those next six years. After we lost the house, I went to an apartment in Onalaska. At that point, Scott had become violent. He threw me into the wall, almost broke my neck, and my arm was fractured. It was so unlike him. He was not that type of guy. He didn't even raise his voice, so this was all the tumor. It was so scary! It was tough, but we just couldn't make it work," Jana said. "We just had so many outside stressors. For Scott, recovering from the surgery took a long time. I tried to be there for him with that, but it just took its toll on both of us."

"When he threw me into the wall and hurt me, I couldn't work so I left my job. My son was working at Red Lobster at the time trying to pay the rent. But it just didn't work, so we lost our apartment. That's when Scott and I broke up and just ended things."

"Because we lost the apartment, my son and I lived in our Oldsmobile Bravada. It was nice because we could put the seats down at night. I loved that Bravada. That's the last vehicle I ever owned. We tried to live in it for about three years. It was difficult, yes, but my family would let us sleep on the couch sometimes, or stay with them for a little while," Jana said.

"However, my son and I were using drugs together, so no one wanted us around. We still stayed together. Neither one of us left the other, you know. We were going to see this through. It was like this," Jana shared, "We felt close and connected like, *'You're my mom!' 'You're my son!'* Fast forward to the year 2019. This is where my real homeless story begins." "Your son is thirty years old now," I said, "So when you two left the Bravada, where did you go?"

Jana elaborated, "When we left the Bravada, it was because we couldn't afford to maintain it anymore. It was breaking down and had tickets from parking places. I had never been homeless before, so it was difficult to know the things I could or couldn't do. I hadn't ever experienced having bills left unpaid! We hadn't ever experienced life with no power in our home or no heat, nothing like that. I never had to worry about getting evicted."

I responded to Jana, "It was very strange for you, I see, and new to you and your son to be in this situation. You managed in the vehicle, but even that was a stressor to be in a van all the time. Then when the vehicle, which was your home, needed repairs, it cost money that you didn't have. It seemed to mount around you uncontrollably." Jana agreed, "Yes! But we were so addicted to drugs that we didn't even want to work! By then, it was about 2015 and I met a guy who was a drug dealer. He dealt a lot of drugs around the area, a lot!" she emphasized.

"He had three kids. One was an infant so I was their nanny, kind of, for a little while. His wife and I were friends. But his wife left him," Jana said. "Okay, so back to the kids. He had three kids, a baby, a seven-year-old, and a nine-year-old. That was hard, too, because their mom just left them! She left and just walked away! Here I am, raising three kids for about three years," she said. "So from 2016 to 2019, that's where I was," I asked her if she lived with the family as a nanny and received an income for it as well. "Yep," she answered. "Okay, yeah, but then he and I started to see each other. We began a relationship after they got divorced. I helped raise the kids for three years while he dealt drugs. It was just chaotic!" Jana explained. "We rarely fought or anything like that, but he just had a lot of things about him that I didn't like. I had to get out of there. So, we broke up in 2019."

Jana continued her story, "That's when I met Scott number two." Jana said that her son, Devin, had met a young woman named Anita who had an apartment on Island Street. "It was a teeny tiny little efficiency apartment upstairs. But after a couple of days, Devin and I got into a big argument and he took all my clothes, all my stuff, and threw it off the balcony. I was down there trying to pick it all up, you know. I was trying to stuff it into my bags and I'm crying my eyes out!"

"This guy, who I saw at someone's house before, came up and asked what was going on and whether I needed help. *'Yes! I don't know where I'm going! I don't know what to do!'* I told him that I'd never been in all this before. At this point, I knew I would be outside because I'd already been in the vehicle and on couches. So this was it! You wouldn't think it would go lower, but every step of the way, things got worse and worse and worse! Along the way, I look up and there's Scott number two!"

"He's the guy who was helping me get my clothes and things together! *'I'll show you where to go, where you can get food. I'll show you where you can stay at night when it's cold,'* he said." I asked Jana if this man was unhoused also. "Is that why he knew everything?" I questioned. Jana answered, "Yeah, he was and he knew everything! He was awesome! There was instantly this strong pull that we had for each other. So, from that day on, good things happened!"

But then Jana said, "He passed away! He died just four years ago in 2020. We met in April of 2019 and I lost him in August 2020," she said sadly. "I never loved anyone. I didn't love Scott number one nearly as much as I love Scott number two. He was so smart, so kind. I never met anybody like him. He made me a better person."

"Life leading up to that point made me angry and bitter. I thought I had to fight everybody and that the world was against me. But he was so kind. He had been a youth minister for his dad up north in Spooner, Wisconsin. But he moved down here to La Crosse. I don't know why, but his sister lived here. We never really talked about that."

Jana shared how she advanced to shooting up meth. "That's when I started shooting because Scott did. That's what he did." I asked her if this had caused Scott's death. "Yeah. Okay, but yeah, he taught me about bikes, so we loved bikes. We rode, I swear, to every corner in the city. Because we were homeless, we had nothing else to do but ride around all day and night! So we rode all over this town," Jana said.

"He was my everything! Because of COVID, the needle exchange was closed, so we were using our dirty needles. I remember making his shot for him and, when I looked at it, I saw a plug of dry blood in the shot. I told him, *'You can't do this!'* but he did it anyway," she said as she lowered her head.

"It was only a few hours later that he…this was at the end of June. A few hours later, he had a high fever and different areas of his body were hurting. We thought it was because we had just walked for three days straight, just straight around town. It was summer and nice but, oh, he was so sick. We didn't live anywhere in town at the time. We just knew people who had houses, or we would just sleep outside. It was summer and then, in the winter, we would go to the warming shelter. So we were staying in a friend's house on the island (*note: French Island is located off the banks of the Mississippi River on the northwest side of La Crosse*). We knew Mike, so he let us stay there. I have so many memories of that place," Jana was deep in thought and looked down as she spoke.

"It's where we got engaged. We got engaged in the bathroom with this crazy drug dealer named Rat and his crazy girlfriend. They were arguing and I was sitting on the toilet while they were standing there. Scott was over here and he just says, *'Put up your hand here,'* in the middle of all this, those two bickering, and I said, *'What?'* Heather said, *'Did he just, are you just, is this happening!?'* Then Scott said, *'Yep!'* "I was shocked, *'Oh, my God! Yep!'* It was so amazing! That was 2019 on his birthday, August 18, 2019, when we got engaged."

"So when he got sick a year later, we wanted to make sure we were together if we knew he was that sick. They said he was the sickest man in the hospital! He had sepsis and myocarditis, that's inflammation of the heart mitral valve," Jana explained, "And it was causing little clots to break off. They were shooting holes in his organs! They were breaking off inside his body! Then he had a stroke! I could see that he was so sick," she said sadly, "My gosh, he would just scream! With sepsis, we didn't know what the warning signs were, and here we'd been walking for three days. We thought his back pain and foot pain were from walking, but it was, oh my God, he was bleeding internally! Ohhh, it was so severe!"

I tried to reassure Jana by saying, "We all do this. We think and hope it's something more average, more tolerable, and something we can overcome." She continued, "But the foot pain was because he wasn't getting circulation to his feet," Jana cried. "We didn't even look at his feet! If we had, maybe, I don't know, but just when we got to the hospital, his toes were black. No blood or fluid. He was in the hospital for thirty-three days!" Jana said.

I was surprised that he had survived that long after Jana said, "During his first three days in the hospital, they removed his spleen but wouldn't give him pain medication because he was an addict. So I yelled at them," she said. "I told them, *'If you don't give him something stronger than Tylenol, I'm going to go out on the street and get it for him!'* because he was just lying there screaming!" I asked Jana, "After that, did they give him something or did you have to find something?" She did not answer but a great deal of emotion was released throughout her story.

Jana said, "Ohh my goodness, it was just four years ago, and it is coming up. Oh, my God, at the end of June through the entire month of July, I couldn't go back to that apartment. He had two strokes and open heart surgery. They removed a valve and put in a replacement valve. A week later, they wanted to discharge him. But he couldn't go back out on the streets! You know, he wasn't stable!"

I asked Jana, "Do you know why they wanted to release him against your wishes?" She said, "Over the last four years, I've come to think that maybe the doctors knew he was dying. He wasn't going to make it and they didn't..." she trailed off. After a moment of thought, she said, "So they just, well, if it was to a person's house, they'd send him home. But a homeless person, what do they think? Are they supposed to release them, just discharge them? They wouldn't keep him anymore, which I don't understand. I know people who have had endocarditis and other heart conditions from drugs and they are in the hospital for..." Jana stopped talking mid-sentence as she pondered Scott's end of life four years ago. "I don't know why," she said quietly. "Scott was a person. He believed. He believed in something greater in the world. More than signs from the universe and things like that. He was always trying to teach me things and, during that time, he was trying to tell me things."

She continued, "I was trying to get his things together and listen to the nurses. They were saying everything about what medications when, and how to do everything. How to take care of his incisions and the little bags, you know, little drainage bags and stuff. So we had all these little things that I had to take care of and tons of medication. I had to know about diet, too."

"On his birthday," Jana said with a smile, "Scott ate his entire cake. *'It's my birthday!'* he said. But then he got sick and we needed to go to the hospital. Thank God for Julie because she had Econo Lodge. Scott woke up with a 105° fever. I called upstairs for the nurse to come down or to call an ambulance because they told me, that if he had a high fever, call an ambulance right away! Because it would mean the infection was back."

"I stayed at the hospital nearly every single night for thirty-three nights, except for two nights because the doctor told me to take a break. Every day, they told me I shouldn't be there, but I did anyway. *'I'm not leaving!'* I told them, *'I'm the only one he's got!'* His family lives up north. He had no will. But we got married in the hospital. After his spleen was removed, before his big heart surgery, we had the whole hospital talking about it! It was just Scott, me, and the priest. We said some type of thing and he set up the prayer. The state had something for us to sign, but we had so much going on, that he couldn't get it done. Scott couldn't leave the hospital but we were going to pay for a real wedding official. But we didn't get one," Jana said sorrowfully. I told her, "You got married in heart and spirit though." She said, "Yep. And in my mind, legally."

"I can't imagine never hearing his voice again and never holding his hand again. Never!" Jana said, "It's been a long five years since he died," I added, "Hasn't it, with such longing and grief about what happened to you and Scott? I hope that you were there when he died. You were there the entire time otherwise."

Jana continued with this devastating story. "I thought I had to call another hospital. He had two strokes at the house on Island Street. We'd gotten engaged, but he had two strokes there. So I called and he did go. A friend of ours let us spend a couple of nights only two blocks from the hospital, near the university."

My phone died and all I could think was, *'he's going to be in the hospital again. I need to call his parents, that's all, his parents.'* I wanted to let his sister know, and my son know, that he's in the hospital now. But my phone was dead, so I had to walk back to my friend Stuart's to get my charger. Meanwhile, Scott kept telling me that he wanted to leave the hospital. But I said, *'No, you need to be here! If you leave, you're going to die! You need to be on an IV,'* but he kept saying, *'No, I just want to go home! I just want to go home! I just want to go lay down!'* I yelled at him, *'Clearly you need to be here!"*

The doctor asked to start the process for the power of attorney because Scott wasn't making medical decisions for himself. It's the process that makes me able to make decisions for him so he doesn't sign himself out. I told him I'd be right back, and I did come back twenty minutes later. But Scott had left the hospital. He just walked out!"

Part two of Jana's story about what happened to Scott and more about her life in La Crosse is continued at the end of the section.

RYAN MARKS

RYAN MARKS and I met in Tent City. When I asked if he wanted to tell his story, Ryan said he did and would like to tell it right then, but without his picture included. He said, "Yeah, it is better to tell it without knowing your face will be on it." I showed him my phone screen where his words appeared in text as it typed across the page, "to assure you that they are your words, not mine or anyone else making up what you're saying." Ryan settled and seemed open to talking about himself, seemingly for the first time in a very long time.

I told Ryan that I wanted to know how he traveled to Tent City today while living outdoors alone. "You are not that old to have a long history out here, are you?" I asked. "I'm thirty-one," he answered. "I am thirty-one years old." He was handsome, noticeably groomed, and nicely dressed in what appeared to be clean and maintained clothes. His hair was combed and trimmed. All of this is unexpected for people living unhoused, with few resources, while battling weather and the outdoor elements full-time. Besides his physical appearance, I saw that Ryan's face was filled with emotion, but I couldn't interpret what I sensed.

"What happened to you that brought you to live out here?" I asked. Ryan elaborated, "I've been homeless a lot in my life, even as a child. As a child but, you know, becoming an adult, I was homeless. I lived on the streets, and back then, I didn't look at it as homeless, you know."

I questioned if he had always been in La Crosse or if he had been in other cities, too. "Yeah, the whole time, in La Crosse," he said. Ryan continued to explain that he was born in La Crosse and that this was the lifestyle he had always known. "I was, kind of, raised into drugs and to do drugs, you know." When I asked him to elaborate on whether his family raised him in the drug world, he said, "Oh yeah, in a way, yeah." He agreed that, if a person is born into a different family, their choices would be differ. "But that's what you knew," I said. "Yeah," he said, "and it's not just what I knew, but what I was, I'd say, I guess, or what I was allowed to do and encouraged to do, to be able to support myself and my family."

"What do you feel about it?" I asked. "Pain," he said so quietly that I barely heard his voice. "Pain," Ryan repeated, nodding his head but looking off across the river, tears welling in his eyes. "You look as though you feel that pain right now and very much," I said, "and I do, too. I feel it for you as we talk because I see how difficult it is for you. It is complicated and hard to get out of addiction once you get into it. What have you done with anyone in the services here in town to work toward getting into recovery? Has it been available for you?" I asked. "Ohh, I've tried," Ryan said, "but it's just, it's hard for me. I did. I got myself together for a while, yeah. I had a family."

When I asked if he had children, Ryan said he had two with his girlfriend, the mother of his children. After a few minutes of silence, I asked him what happened between him and his family. Tears spilled down his cheeks as he continued, "I'm just, I'm just...I don't know. I guess I couldn't change. I was, I wasn't good enough. And I lost my family because of it."

We talked together about how drugs can snare a person and not release them. I suggested that "the feeling of not being good enough is just the emotional experience. But the truth is, you are good enough," I told him. "Addiction is what you do or what has happened to you, but the inner stuff is who you are as a person. You are still Ryan, with hopes and desires. You are young, and you can experience change, despite how it feels." Ryan shared how impossible it felt to have hope. He said, "I bet my family doesn't even love me in their life unless I'm doing what I can to take care of it." But it was clear that Ryan could barely care for himself, let alone his family.

I asked him if he ever had known what he wanted for his life or what he wanted to do. He answered, "I had to care for my bills, support my family, and even my nieces and nephews. But I have a couple of business ideas, you know. Nothing, I know, it's not going to get me rich," he conceded. "What are your business ideas?" I asked. "Oh, well, one of them is a food truck. It should, if it goes well, you know, I don't think anybody's had the idea before." I questioned whether he likes to cook, and he replied, "Yeah! I randomly think about some things, and I have good ideas. Like absolutely just random stuff that won't get me rich, but it'll help support...don't need to be rich, but just to support my family," he trailed off, wiping tears from his face.

We discussed how he did not need to become rich but only to have enough to keep a home and support his family. He agreed that his desire to change was a big hurdle he had already overcome. "I want to change," he said, "But it feels impossible. I don't know what to do." Because he wanted to change and had dreams and ideas about what he could do, he was a step ahead. I commented that a food truck is an achievable goal, especially at his age.

"You have a drug addiction. I realize that. It is out here in abundance, and it can keep you stuck right where you are, pulling you down and holding you back," I said. Ryan agreed that the drugs help a person feel steady, but, at the same time, it keeps them from growing more stable, he told me. "It's an enormous problem, isn't it?" I asked. Ryan continued, "Yeah, drugs got bad these past two years. Yeah, you know it's become just an addiction, just like you're a slave to it. Yeah. I was able to maintain and support...I was even...I'd work a job, but I'd sell drugs, too."

Ryan described his hopelessness. Without hope, he knew that he could not prevail over homelessness, unemployment, family loss, or drug addiction. It was a hopeless cycle and he didn't feel able to get out of it.

I explained the Karuna House to Ryan and told him five people were on each side of the duplex. He had vaguely heard about it but without knowing any specific details. I told him it was a pilot program for people previously experiencing homelessness. Some were sober, and others were working on it.

There is help and support, and it doesn't risk the tenants' ability to stay at Karuna if they haven't fully recovered yet. This model respects the difficulty and challenges associated with recovery. "Karuna offers a home without the threat of loss due to relapse and what is often seen as a failure during recovery," I explained. Ryan said he would appreciate a situation like Karuna for himself. He agreed to keep watch for future arrangements for similar housing situations.

Ryan had plenty of love for his family as well as an abundance of sorrow for how he had disappointed them and for the losses in his life. He had ideas and desires for the future, which included being a strength and help to his family. Before we parted that day, Ryan shared that he has two sisters and two brothers besides his two children and their mother, and he said that he is aware that his addiction has pushed them away and they have pushed him away. Hopelessness filled his voice as he trailed off and continued to cry. He said that he believes they will never come back together again. He agreed, though, that his primary relationship at this time was with his addiction, in its struggle and battle, which he acknowledged as he walked away with his head hanging.

Thank you, Ryan, for the courage to tell your story.

PHILIP LAVENDUSKEY (BUBBA)

PHILIP LAVENDUSKEY (BUBBA) and I discussed his life. I told him, " You have told me a lot about yourself before today, and I have learned more as I listened to you speak with others. I know your name is Philip, even though you go by Bubba."

"I love the story of your brother mispronouncing 'brother' and saying 'Bubba,' instead. That is how you got the nickname 'Bubba' as a child. I'd like to hear about your early childhood, and when you were a boy. Do you have memories you'd like to share?"

Bubba began, "My memories are failing. I'm sorry." He continued to explain, "I have a memory problem. My grandmother had it, my brothers, and all my cousins. It skips a generation. I figured my grandmother had nine kids, so those nine had at least one or two children. Of those nine siblings, my aunts and uncles, we have memory problems in the family."

"How many siblings do you have?" I asked. "From my mother, I have siblings. From my father, I have a brother. I have the one that passed away." Bubba continued to think about his family and count aloud the number of siblings. When asked if he was the family's youngest, he explained, "No, I'm the middle," as he continued counting his family members. "Of my brothers, Robert is the eldest, from my dad's previous marriage. Oh, ok, so he's my stepbrother, yeah, so I am the oldest other than my half-sister. All but one are alive. The others are still all alive, yeah."

"What do you remember about growing up and having all those kids around?" I asked. Bubba said, "I didn't have them all around, no! I was lonely! It was hard growing up. At thirteen, I was a fat boy, four-foot two-inches tall and 212 lbs." When I asked him if he was bullied because of it, he closed his eyes, leaned back, and sighed, "Ohh, yeah, yeah! I didn't get past junior high!" He expressed sadness about the loss of his young years, from growing up in a dysfunctional family, failing school, and being a victim of bullying. "I got my GED in jail," he said. "I was there for a six-month term, and I thought, *'I might as well do something with my time!'* I probably passed, but they had me in the class. I have good intellect," he said. "Yes, that's a good way to put it," I agreed. "I don't know," Bubba said as he hung his head in his hands.

"Did you have any dreams about your life or what you wanted to become when you were young?" I asked. "No, I never knew," he said. "I still don't know. I want to help people. They can't help themselves, you know!" He continued, "I started protecting myself. I was starved for attention because every time I got attention, it was when I was bad. I wasn't a bad kid growing up. I just did stupid things. Don't get me wrong, but I noticed that *'hey, I'm going to try to get the best attention,'* and I knew I'd get it if I did something bad! My dad was always out, and my mom was at work, so I was the only one at home. I would come home to an empty house but I wanted attention. I didn't want to do my homework so I never did it. There was always something better to do. I could learn, but I didn't want to."

"You didn't have the parenting you needed to make that happen. Not every kid would do their home-work when no one was around to encourage them? You didn't have a healthy functional upbringing that would teach you to make those choices," I answered. Bubba continued about his family. "Right! My parents were spending money, so I thought maybe she'd use some for her kids. Well, here are both kids, one at school and one in daycare. Well, what do you think happened then?" he said. "I had to leave the house and become a grown-up when I was fifteen years old! But I had raised two very good boys, my younger brothers. When I left, I should not have left those boys," Bubba said as tears ran down his face. "I was gone for six years after that. When I returned, my brothers asked, *'Where did you go?'* I told them I went to Oregon. They were grown by then, and past knowing me. They missed me, but it wasn't the same anymore."

Like so many others living in the unsheltered community, Bubba experienced years of loss beginning in childhood and continuing throughout his adulthood. He seemed to carry much guilt and grief about the complexities that brought him along this path. "I still figure I did it wrong," Bubba continued. "I was told to leave and never come back. I was twenty-five years old at the time. When my dad first threw me out, it was because we got into an argument. He said, *'Don't come back!'* So I didn't. That first night after we fought, I slept in a shed at a farmhouse. The worst time of my life was probably when I was thirteen."

Bubba told a story of trauma that happened when he was only thirteen. "I watched my friend die in my arms after she did a line of coke that had glass in it. She was murdered and was only sixteen years old. I loved her! I believed she was my soul mate." Bubba said, "I've been on the streets most of my life. I try to be nice, but my whole life is mostly about survival. Even today, I am trying to survive. But I want to do what's right."

Expanded on his experience living at the Karuna House in La Crosse, Bubba explained how he could wake up, have his needs met, eat three times a day, rest, and not have to live at risk as he has in the past while on the streets. He wants to learn to organize his belongings and keep his room in order. Living with others has helped him learn about community development and shared efforts.

He told about an incident when he and another person in the house had a conflict. Bubba could read the situation, he said, and attempt constructive conflict resolution to repair the problem between them. He felt pleased to be able to get clear about the other person's role, too. "Everything in the house becomes an opportunity," Bubba said, "of things I had never learned before."

Changing the subject, Bubba revealed, "I'm going to be fifty years old in July!" "Well, that's not too old to dream or hope for something new for your future. Look where you are now compared to last season. You now have a home, regular food, housemates, friends, a room and bed, a bathroom, and medical support." I said. Bubba replied, "I only dream about the next day. I'm happy when I wake up in the morning because I made it. I made it to the next day!" he said. "I am young, but I have an old spirit and soul. I miss my childhood, and I missed my childhood!" When I asked Bubba if he does anything fun for himself, he said, "I like video games. I have a lot of fun when I play."

I witnessed Bubba's leadership skills when he escorted me to Tent City during my first visits there. He was careful and watchful as he showed me around and introduced me to people who lived there or who were passing through. He took it upon himself to monitor my time there and notify me when I was to leave for another appointment. I told him I had noticed these skills and asked if he knew he had them. His reply was, "I'm not worthy. Somewhere, somebody out there is better. There's someone out there who is better than me. I'm no leader. I'm no leader!" Bubba said that he believed he couldn't be a leader since he still needed to be led.

"I do have values, yeah. Morals, good morals, and character. I have a good heart. But I have someone inside me who beats me up, so I'll never think of myself as worthy. Never." I reminded him that, at forty-nine, he has a long future ahead to feel unworthy or to learn about feeling worthy. After I suggested that he might challenge those thoughts, Bubba replied, "I don't really, I can't! I'm a drug addict. Drug addicts are not worthy. Oh. The shame. I feel sad because I'm taking from somebody else," Bubba said with tears running down his face. "I've taught myself this, so I tell myself I am taking from others."

When I reminded him he admittedly values helping others, he said, "I guess. I don't look at it the same way other people do." Bubba revealed much about his life and feelings and then expressed sadness and guilt. As we finished our conversation, I thanked him. He left to take a walk and have a cigarette.

Thank you, Bubba, for courageously sharing your story for this book. Your consistent help with the interviewing process is also much appreciated.

HEATHER ARCHER

HEATHER ARCHER is a former Houska Park camper and a member of the Lived Experience Team. She is well-known at Tent City and Karuna House, where she helps others in any way she can. Heather can be seen carrying a backpack filled with various supplies that come in handy to those living outdoors at any given time. She is always prepared to assist with a spare cigarette, clean needle, water, extra food, Narcan, or a sweatshirt on a chilly day. She will give whatever she has if, as she says, "they need it more than I do."

Heather begins her life story in 1998 when she was named *'patient zero'* in a bacterial meningitis case. She started, "My mother is like you," she said while looking at me and assessing my height. "She is shoulder status to me. But she carried me into the Henry County Health Center over her shoulder after she found me lying face down on our front porch in the morning." I asked, "How old were you?" Heather replied, "I'd have to do the math. I was born in '83, and it was '98, yeah," Heather gave it more thought. "I was as tall and big as I am now but I was fifteen years old. My little mother did that! Yeah, wow! My mother did that!"

"Strange thing," Heather said. "She picked me up and carried me into that hospital! When I got there, my temperature was 107.3° Fahrenheit, which is active brain dead. My neural pathways were like fire in the brain. They were burning away. I asked, "How long were you in that condition?" Heather replied, "I think it was seven and a half hours. I was dying! I don't know what the doctor said since this is second-hand information because I don't remember it myself. They used a dialysis machine to pump the blood out of my body, cool it down, and pump it back in. They had my body on ice."

"I think that I was the first recorded patient zero. Those who lived were on something like that, and I might be wrong, but I know at least in that area, everybody just kept restarting my heart! They used ice to cool my body, and then my heart stopped. I was dying. I was dying because everything was cooking my body. It isn't designed to be at that temperature, but once they got me stable, like my heartbeat and my body functioning again, I went into a coma for about two weeks."

I asked questions about Heather's amazing survival, "Did they put you in the coma, or did you..." "No," she interjected, "I naturally went into a coma! They told my mom things like, you know, *'remove her from all life support. She's not going to be...'* I'm not going to be me! Brain damage, you know. Doctors did not think it was even possible." She said, "But I woke up two weeks later! My mother gave it to God and waited. And then I woke up two weeks later. I had full-grade amnesia."

"I don't have any memories from the first fifteen years of my life." Her story continued as Heather tells how her brain recovered. "It wasn't that the information wasn't there. I started building different pathways. I'm looking at the sunlight, and I'm not understanding, but then the brain restarts to process light, which kicks in the information there. But I don't have the same connection to it."

"How do you see this impacting your life now as an adult?" I asked. Heather responded, "I think being able to understand other people. I'm constantly on the fence – I see it that way and this way. I've gotten good at giving it some grace, and that's a direct consequence of my life experience and it's a good thing. People get in their way, and I don't think I'm doing any better than anybody else. I'm just different. I think everybody gets up every day and does the best that they can, with their limitations."

"I still battle myself. I am still human in every way that matters. But I fight myself all the time. We are our own worst critics but we can't help it! A person walks into a room and thinks, *'They're staring at me, oh my goodness!'* You know everybody feels that way. Yeah, human things like that have happened in my life. It has just given me a different pair of glasses," Heather said, "I'm just a little bit kinder to people around me now."

"We're born unable to care for ourselves at the beginning, so we cry as an infant to get the attention. We are born learning how to manipulate just to survive. We are born selfish because, otherwise, we wouldn't be able to even live," Heather explained.

I interrupted and said, "You sound like a philosopher, a seeker in how you see and think about life." Heather replied, "I just have a different perspective. The medical trauma affected my life and how I connected to it again, to those traumatic events in my early life," Heather admitted.

"I've spoken to you about me and my baby daddy and how we just bounce off each other. We create a wrecking ball," she reminded me. "It's so human! I will cause damage and don't feel bad like other people typically do. But I'm getting up and doing the best I can. I am flawed, and I am a pain. God has got to be sitting up there saying, *'You've done it wrong twenty times! Stop it!'* But I keep saying, *'I'm flawed!'* That's a huge thing to say," she smiled.

"They say the definition of insanity is doing the same thing repeatedly but looking for different results. That's me!" Heather laughed. "That's my title! I am insane, then! I'm stubborn, and that's a good trait, but it can turn on you. But it's good that it gets you through all sorts of dysfunction, too."

Heather teared up as she thought about something else. She began to talk about the raising of children. "What do I want them to learn from it? I'm learning new coping skills and resilience now. I'm trying to dump everything that I get now into those kids! I drive my daughter nuts," she grinned.

I reminded Heather, "I met your daughter at your house. She was telling about the bus ride home, remember, and I thought she was quite dimensional and seemed articulate for being only nine." She nodded and said, "Every parent is here doing the best they can. I live by some of those fundamentals, although I don't always get them right, especially if I'm all up in my feelings. I'm like a five-year-old and just so reactionary! I see it in myself, and I see it in others."

Heather was open about being in counseling in the local health system. She explained something she learned. "You know, put space between it. This is your feelings," and she motioned with one hand. "Nothing in your feelings is wrong. We are entitled to that feeling. We can feel it in any way. Then we have thoughts," she said as she motioned with her other hand, "and over here, we have actions. This space is supposed to be between them. The problem is, as humans, we are good at feeling reaction-feeling-reaction! That's not how it's supposed to be," Heather said before briefly pausing to wipe tears from her eyes. Then she continued, "We're never going to get control. We're never going to get that 100% right as humans. We are our own worst enemy," she said with a smile and a glance toward me.

"Wow," Heather seemed to surprise herself with her insights and continued, "but our brain chemicals make us feel fight or flight. Our hearts start beating as we become angry - that's chemistry, yeah, yeah," she nodded affirmingly. "I say to people, *'Man, life sucks, humans suck.'* But God gives us grace every day," she said softly.

Tears ran slowly from Heather's eyes as she resumed, "One of the things I don't, well, it's hard to accept is that..." she began to cry as she showed her grief. "I lost my son, and it's easy to say, *'how can life, how can God...?'* but what does that serve? What higher power...?" She trailed off. "But still, why did it happen?"

"Everything is complicated, while everything is so simple, at the same time, but still so complicated. I want to be this force that makes beauty and good for others," Heather concluded.

Thank you, Heather, for sharing your depth of experience and thoughts.

GREG

GREG started his story, "I lived in La Crosse until I was fifteen years old. My family moved around a lot when I was younger. My family included my brother, sister, and my mom. We're all five years apart. I met my father when I was little and then once when I was fifteen. I also had a few different stepdads because it was hard for a single mom trying to raise the three of us. I was not the easiest one to raise. I was wild!" Greg said with a smile.

I asked if he was the oldest. He answered, "Yes, I was the oldest so I got to see and experience a little bit of everything throughout our life. I saw the whole shebang of everything, you know? I learned a lot and lived a lot. Mom did the best she could with what she knew. My mom lives in Owatonna, Minnesota so we talk periodically. I am reminded now that I should give her a call."

"It sounds like a while since you two have spoken," I said. Greg replied, "Yeah, yeah, ohh yeah! I love Mom. I mean, she was the best mom in my eyes! She did the best that she could with what she knew. How she was raised...she had a rough life growing up so that doesn't help. But Mom knew right from wrong and she was young while trying to raise kids. She still had help from her mom, a little bit," he explained.

Greg continued to reflect on these two important women in his early life. "My grandma was amazing! She had ten kids, including twins who passed away. This was a sad deal back then." Greg stopped for a minute while considering what he just said. "So there were eight of them all together then. I remember Grandma spoiling me rotten," he smiled. "I came and went as I wanted." When I asked if his grandma was still living, Greg said, "She's been gone for quite a while now. Her family was a little rough around the edges."

"You're a very smiley person," I commented, "for having such a rough start and being raised by people who had difficult times." Greg answered, "Yeah, but you need to take the good with the bad and just go with it. I learned a lot growing up though, I mean some of it I don't wish upon anybody, and some of it is just the way life went. The rest of it, well, I was that kid that was just a little happy, very energetic in everything, you know? I was in many places I shouldn't have been, places I obviously wouldn't have my kids go! I knew everything and I survived! I am forty-five years old," Greg revealed.

"You were fifteen when you left home," I said. "That's thirty years you have been on your own." Greg answered, "There was a lot of transitioning in my early teens. We moved a lot when I was younger. I went to multiple different schools. Sometimes I changed schools two or three times in one year! I had to jump around from here to there and meet new people all the time while trying to adapt and re-adapt. I would get new friends but it was hard to fit. I was the oddball kid when these other kids already knew each other and were friends. I was always the oddball so I never really knew where I stood, you know? They already were acclimated to each other because they had known each other since childhood. Here I am, the new guy, always the new guy. I guess, for me, it made me kind of a people person. I had to become that as a way of survival. I had to learn how to talk to people very quickly or try to make new friends instantly. I never totally fit in, or knew where I stood in life," Greg said. "I'm very well-rounded with everybody."

Greg continued to explain some of his thoughts about people. "Everybody has a uniqueness within themselves. I never really stood up for just certain types. I stood up for everybody if it was right. I was the odd one, in a sense, and I had to feel all these cliques all the time, constantly. It caused me to learn how to adapt in the best way that I knew how. It was normal that I didn't know what was going on in my life. I would be told, *'We're going to move again,'* because of money issues or it would be Mom's relationships. She had a lot of work stuff, just a lot going on," Greg explained.

When I asked if he was ever able to complete school, he said, "That was quite the challenge, yeah, very challenging. It's hard for a kid to, you know, finish. I was so high-strung that I couldn't sit still in school. For me to learn, you know, and then move around from here to there to here, so many different schools, that was a little rough," he said. "I was a young age when I had a learning disability. I called it extremely hypersensitive. I was very hyperactive - ADHD kind of stuff in a sense. I was very smart in my mind but I couldn't concentrate. I couldn't focus on reading and words. All the numbers were like gibberish. It still is like this to this day and I know it is a little bit wrong. You can't corral that on your own," he said. "It's just so much to take as a kid because I'm taking in everyone's feelings. It's just a very hypersensitive way I've always been. I don't know whether it's just in the genes or where it comes from exactly. But it's something that became an impasse."

Greg continued, "Nobody picked up what I was going through. I just dealt with it. There was so much going on inside me that I couldn't control it. What happened in the two decades of my twenties and thirties to where I am now, all these years I have been out, living from place to place.

I moved out of Wisconsin when I was fifteen years old. It was a tough transition for me because I had a lot of friends in La Crosse and finally felt rooted. My friends and I were rough and tough, rowdy. We were the cool kids!" Greg smiled widely. "No one told us what to do or we'd bust. I tried to be that kind of guy and was that guy a little bit. But I just felt so bad. It was just that it was life, at the time. We were kids growing up," he explained.

"When I met my father, I was fifteen years old. I was with a Christian family, the Woods family. They took me in for a while because previously we went to church in Sparta. They did a lot with me over the years, church-based things, and I got to know God. I was involved in learning about the Lord and Christianity. I got to know about the righteous way of life which I had not seen until that family took me in. I was able to feel it since and it was a different lifestyle for me from about age ten or eleven to my mid-teens. I spent summers there so, during that part of my life, I got to experience many different things, from every aspect. It was not the kind of stuff I knew in my family. But I needed it and I had it. So I have had a lot of that in me. Mom tried to get us to church once in a while. So having me in church at that age, I opened up some. I was able to experience that righteous side of life and believe it," Greg explained.

"I went to youth groups and was in Royal Rangers which was like Boy Scouts but church-based. I went to Bible camp and Fort McCoy to the gym. I also went swimming with the Woods family, which included Josh and Jonathan. I haven't talked to them in years because I don't know exactly where they are located. They were missionaries so they'd travel to Hawaii and had a cabin near Spencer Lake."

Greg continued about his experience with the family that had taken him in. "They decided that they would visit a relative in Sacramento, California. My dad was in California so the Woods family asked if I wanted to meet my father for the first time. Because I was fifteen, I felt nervous about it. I always wanted to meet my father, when I was younger, and always wondered what it would be like to have my biological father in my life. I had not experienced that, but instead was able to experience other kids' fathers and families. I never had that normalcy myself. My *'normal'* was different. I was always longing for somebody else's attention, and trying to grab onto something."

As he opened up more about his family experiences, Greg elaborated on the emotions that rose while with those who took care of him. "I could feel some of the tension between the fathers and their children. Sometimes it got to the point that they didn't feel sorry for me, but they realized that I was not needy, but I was very understanding. Eventually, the parents in other families accepted me as one of theirs. They wanted to adopt me. Many families felt like this, which caused me to realize how natural it was for me, a very natural thing, that I could exude warmth and love."

Greg said that he felt this when he came to Karuna House. "People want that," he said. "They want humility and kindness for the most part. Don't get me wrong, I can get grouchy sometimes, just like anybody, but I'd rather just be kind and relaxed. Before Karuna, I was out on the streets and at the warming center. I also lived at Houska Park and in other parks, so this is a major shift for me. Major, yes, a major change for me," Greg repeated with a smile. "It's good for me."

"When I decide I'm going to do something, I do it knowing I have control of my life. Drugs and alcohol do not control me, honestly. Even when I was down and out and using, I was still in control. I knew just what I needed to medicate myself, in a sense, very experimental. I was in charge of it, but eventually, I could feel it begin to take control of me. It felt strange as if I was in a different world, you know, and I was up for days. I became sleep-deprived and was not eating properly. It was in this way that it took my control away."

Greg described the difficult experience he had with drug use. While in Tent City, he said that he began to speak, "as though God was speaking through me," he said. During the experience, he was very tired and felt that he needed to take a nap immediately to shut things off. Greg realized he was talking aloud to himself and believed he may have seemed to others around him like he was losing his mind. But somehow he knew he would be all right and was aware he was altered by drug use. He said, "When altered, a person is going to run into feelings that they have...well, I don't have to talk about that right now," he decided, "but it's stuff that makes you feel weird. I got past that point and eventually decided I was stressed to the max. It all sounds fun and games but I was highly medicated, high as a kite, but trying to cover up all of the feelings and emotions while trying to figure out what was going on in my life."

Greg's description of his drug episode was bold and detailed, "What happened is that my whole life passed before me, right in front of my eyes, before I realized it. This was so much for me to take in while, at the same time, I was taking in everybody else's stuff! I was trying to give advice and help the other person at the same time. I didn't know what to say! I knew what I felt right then. I started to miss my kids more than anything in the world! But I knew I couldn't do anything about it," he said with sadness. "It was as if I was stuck in my little bubble, just chaos and craziness and so overwhelming. It's such a sad place to be as it overtakes your mind and body. It's just heart-wrenching and it hurts so bad."

I took a moment to ask Greg how things have changed for him now that he is off the streets and living at Karuna House. "Believe it or not," he replied, "as time went by, I just got to the point where I couldn't do it anymore. I didn't want to do it! This is not who I am! I know who I am and I know who I want to be. But, how am I going to get there? I don't have very many options. I had support from the community and others taking me in. But it is a battle that I need to do all on my own. When I decide I'm done with something, I'm done. If I'm going to do something, I'm going to do it. I'm the one in charge here. This is my body, my mind, and my soul. Granted," he said, "it comes from God, and God is there. But I have to make the big-boy decision to just follow through with it."

Greg turned his focus to his children. "I do not want my kids to ever go through something like I did, or experience it in any way. It's just way too much to even explain to them the heart-wrenching feeling I have." I urged Greg to talk more about his children and where they are now. He said, "My son is sixteen and my daughter will be fourteen." When I asked if they were in his life at all, he explained, "It's been over six years now since I've spoken to them. Talking to them is just such a heart-wrenching thing, but I had to grow and get back to being normal again and healthy. I had to be me again. They at least call me *'big daddy.'* They live in Caledonia, Minnesota, not far. It's the worst feeling in the world."

After Greg spoke about his children, I said to him, "Greg, since I met you, each time I see you, you present with strength and a desire to heal. I see where it may possibly come from - your children. Your mom taught you a lot about moving around and being resilient which you've repeated throughout your life. I hear that you don't want your kids to have the same as you have, as their inheritance." Greg responded, "When I left them, there were a lot of reasons why I left, but I knew where they were and where they were going to be safe. I knew they were taken care of. That was good, but there was a lot of tension with my wife. It was just fire and water, very rough." Thinking about Greg's desire to grow and become healthy, I asked him about his job.

"I was working at Pickerman's for a while, the sandwich and soup shop down on Jay Street. He's a great guy and it's a great place. I like food, and I like to eat and cook!" He shared, "I like to cook a little bit, a lot, especially when I'm hungry, I start whipping. If I don't have a lot of stuff to pick from, then I just start to whip easy stuff together to make it good enough." I asked Greg about his love for preparing food and his work at Pickerman's restaurant. "Do you have a dream about working more with food in the future? How might your kids figure into that?"

Greg thought a few seconds and then said, "I want to live the rest of my life for my children. Anything I can do to just be there for them," he said thoughtfully, "and guide them in their path and what they want to do. Going from living outside to Karuna House is stability for me. And it's permanent! People get jobs and do this and do that. But I don't know what to do anymore. It's not that I don't want to work. But I'm worthless! It's just hard to know what is on the path for me to make a living, and make it be something for my children."

I reminded Greg that it was not long ago when he lived in a park. "If I met you in a park and asked what you wanted, you might have said that you wanted shelter but you didn't know how to achieve it. And look where you are now, you have shelter. Karuna House is your home. Maybe in the future, the question about making a living and contributing to your children's lives will be answered, just like your shelter question has been answered now." He smiled, "Then I will introduce you to my kids!" Thank you, Greg, for sharing your awesome story. Keep sharing your wonderful smile! I look forward to meeting your children!

LUCAS DELORENZO

LUCAS DELORENZO and I met late one afternoon in the Karuna House kitchen. He began by spelling his name to be sure it was correct for the interview. "Thank you, I have it right now," I said. Then I asked him, "Do you live at Karuna House or do you have a place of your own?" Lucas explained that he has a place of his own. "Thanks to Barb Pollack and Sue Graf for helping me out," he said.

"I have a studio apartment, an awesome little tiny studio. But I'm not home much," Lucas continued. He explained that he devoted a lot of time to church work and meetings. He agreed that having a home of his own gave him a place to sleep, shower, store his belongings safely, cook, and eat. "I also like to watch my daily wire shows. Those are the things I do at home."

When I asked how long he had been in his apartment, Lucas answered, "Since May 1st, so two weeks ago. I went to the Salvation Army Adult Rehabilitation Center on August 8, 2023, through February 7th of this year. It is a six-month program for recovery, people getting out of jail, or those experiencing homelessness, all kinds of things to strengthen skills," he said. "There's a forty-hour work week of work therapy, they call it. I did that routine, so now I still get up at 6:30 almost every day. They had classes and, after the work therapy classes and recovery meetings, there were Bible studies and mandatory church. I'm okay with mandatory church because I'm a practicing Catholic."

After Lucas explained the changes in his life, I asked him, "In what ways is the Lucas who went into the program different from the Lucas who came out?" He gave it some thought and then said, "Well actually, I say hello and good morning to people now. And the old Lucas, he didn't care. So now I have a structured routine which I did not do before."

Continuing to explain his previous drug use, Lucas said, "I know that it won't be different next time. I learned a little bit of humility. I can't just do that one shot of meth and think, *Just, all right, I'm just going to use this one time. I won't use it at work, or I'm just going to get high this one time after church. And then I'll be fine if I just have fun for a few hours.'* " I asked, "So you're not thinking like that now?" Lucas said, "No, I'm not smarter than the program. I'm not stronger than the meth. I'm just not."

As I wondered more about the program Lucas attended, I asked, "How did you get into this?" He told me, "Dean Ciokiewicz helps run the Next Chapter program here in La Crosse. In early August, he was the speaker at an AA meeting at the Alano Society. His story just compelled me." I replied, "Now *your* story is compelling." "Yeah! This guy had quite the story really, like it was a miracle that he's alive and sober! It was like listening to Father Don Calloway's Conversion Story."

Lucas shared a little about his young adulthood and addiction while living unsheltered. Now, at age thirty-five, he looked back at the years of living on the streets. Before August of 2023, he was living in Tent City and Houska Park along the river. He described how he had lived in many locations outdoors in La Crosse on and off for seven years. He appeared energetic, strong, and healthy for having been only recently housed and clean from drug use.

I remarked about this and noted his smile and friendliness. "You just look like you're doing well." Lucas replied, "I hear that a lot at my cathedral parish. After I came back in February, like a new person to them, I became somebody. I'm no longer willing to give that up. That's what my favorite teacher said. I went to all his classes. I find that very awesome because we just sell ourselves out for nothing. I don't want to do that just to get the dope. We would sell ourselves and now I don't want to give that up," Lucas said. "With what you've overcome," I said, "you could become a leader for others out there, to show the possibilities, as an example to show the way." Smiling, Lucas said, "Yeah, working on that!"

Switching topics, Lucas began to speak about his employment. "I work at Pickerman's full time. I do all the stuff there, all the stuff. The owner is a fellow usher at the Cathedral of Saint Joseph the Workman." Lucas explained that he was fortunate to connect like this and apply for a job at the restaurant.

"Do you work at Pickerman's every day?" I asked. "I was there today," Lucas answered. "And it's my day off. But I went because the lobster bisque and the five-star mushroom soups are my favorite things there to eat!" Lucas said he had been working at Pickerman's since February 12th of this year. I reflected to him, "Lucas, you have a new life, new job, new home, new ways of seeing yourself and things around you. Do you want to tell me about the *'old Lucas'* who you've mentioned?"

Previously pretending to live a spiritual life while shooting up dope in Tent City, Lucas remarked, "I go to church every week. I'm a good Catholic boy. I'm just getting high, and pretending I was living a spiritual existence, while out there getting high. So now it's different. I go to mass ten times a week. I go to Blessed Sacrament Monday through Friday at 8:00 A.M. Thursday is now my day off so I go to the 8:00 A.M. there, and then the noon at the cathedral. I'm at the cathedral for all four weekend masses."

Lucas began to share about his childhood. He was born in Bronxville, New York on September 27, 1988, but his family never lived there. The majority of his upbringing was in New Jersey, specifically Bradley Beach and Ocean Grove. In his youth, Lucas explained that he was a pro gamer and "quite good. Super Smash Brothers Series is very good," he said and then changed the subject. "I fell in love with somebody who was going to the University of Wisconsin at La Crosse so I moved out here. For some reason, that just didn't work out. It was because of that, I got high. Yeah, I got high and that was the end of the story," he said. "I was using drugs since late 2015 until my sober date of July 11, 2023." I asked, "You were not a drug user before the age of twenty-seven?" He said, "I did some weed and drank, but drug use is in my family."

"My mom died of an overdose on July 12, 2016. My brother did four and a half years in prison because of heroin-related and violent things. My dad did cocaine but he's been sober for as long as my younger brother has been alive, so about thirty-four years. My mom's dad was an alcoholic. An uncle on my dad's side did crack for seventeen years. But I moved from New Jersey to here and wasn't around my family to keep me in line. Right around the time I lost my mom, I was getting high. That's when it started getting overkill. But it was after my mom died that it was all the drugs! I wanted them all in the syringe!" he said.

When I asked, "Was that a way to deal with your mom's death?" he said, "That was the excuse I used, yeah." I asked, "When you say *'all the drugs,'* what are you referring to?" Lucas listed them, "Meth, heroin, cocaine, weed, whatever it is, I didn't care, yeah, anything, yeah." When I told him that he looked good after years of excessive drug use, he said, "I'm blessed with good genes, I guess. My mom's mom, my grandmother, is currently ninety-nine and alive in Florida. Her mom made it to ninety-nine. Both of my mom's parents made it to the nineties."

"How old was your mom?" I asked. "She was fifty-one when she died from a heroin overdose out on the porch. My brother found her. That happened in Jersey. I was already here." When I asked whether he went back home when she died, Lucas said, "No. No, I just got high. I wanted to go to that funeral and I wanted to stay here, depending on if I was high. That's the answer to everything. But I didn't even cry for a month after she died. Now it's been a few months since I have. My parents were divorced but they still had a good relationship. My mom's parents still treated my dad like their son-in-law," Lucas smiled.

I questioned Lucas about his siblings and he said, "I have an older sister and a younger brother. I'm in the middle." Lucas explained that he was in touch with his younger brother a little bit. "He's sober for two years, now two and a half. He is still in Jersey. My dad's in Florida. He needs a lung transplant. His life's rough, really, and he's overseeing his mother's last days. My grandma is on her last few. She made it pretty far at ninety-nine."

"My dad has eight siblings so I have a lot of cousins, some I have never met. The other day, I just saw one of my cousins' daughters being confirmed into the Catholic Church. My oldest cousin is about fifty-six now. One of my cousins would be maybe twenty-two or twenty-three. I remember when we used to be kids. I thought those older than me were so cool! They babysat us! There's a whole bunch of us who were born in the eighties. I enjoyed my family back then," Lucas added fondly.

Explaining his education and career goals for the future, Lucas said, "I got an associate's degree in political science. That's what I'm most interested in. My Daily Wire membership. I'm that guy who just wants to talk about politics and religion. And then gaming and falling in love," he said. "What changed that dream," I asked. "Ohh, I stayed until I got high," Lucas said. "So getting high did it, yeah, because once you do that, everything else doesn't matter. Yeah, it takes over your life! But I'm back into the politics game!" he said with energy in his voice.

I asked him, "What is your dream now going forward?" Lucas was very determined in his answer, "To be in the election for the parish council and the cathedral! I think I'll win pretty handily! I'm a pretty endearing sentimental character over there! And then maybe City Council because I think the way the City Council is handling the homeless is absurd and stupid!" When I asked him what he would do differently, Lucas said, "There are only three major politicians in the entire continent who I know of who have done well with the homeless. Danielle Smith, the premier of Alberta in central Canada where the third largest oil reserves in the world are located; Kevin Faulconer, the former mayor of San Diego; and Francis Suarez, the current mayor of Miami. I looked into the data and they're all conservatives and Republicans. Well, not a surprise to me that what they did worked!" Lucas stated.

I encouraged Lucas to explain what they each had done that caused it to be so successful. He elaborated further, "Well, up in Alberta, they took buses to the tent cities and announced, *'All right, you want a place to stay, food, your needs met? Okay, fine, you've got to get on this bus. But you're also going to be in recovery and mental illness treatment.'* And that was mandatory! It worked pretty well!" Lucas said. "Would that be a model in all three of these cities," I asked. "In San Diego, they did. In all three of these areas...Alberta is a big province in northern Canada...they got the government out of the way. There's a whole bunch of building codes and zoning regulations and all that," Lucas said.

"The chief executive can use an executive order to just get rid of what Mayor Mitch Reynolds did here temporarily for Houska Park, for example. In San Diego, they started building little housing units, really tiny housing things, after they cleared out the tent city. Instead of doing that over and over and over and over again and locking them up, which all costs money, they just spent the money on that instead. In this area, the regulations to make it cheap could happen. Take away those codes and zoning things, and it becomes cheaper to build."

I asked Lucas, if he was in charge, would he do that here in La Crosse. "Yeah, I think that would be great! But it's hard to get Democratic governance out of the way," he explained. "In the San Diego thing, they had to pay $250 a month rent. Some low numbers like that, but they were hooked up with part-time jobs, community stuff, and little community meals. Somebody would be responsible for making a meal for everybody."

I questioned, "Isn't that kind of like Karuna House here?" Lucas replied "Maybe. I mean this might be an example of it in this town. Governments are not involved. It's community. It has done well except there is the mandatory recovery, mental illness, substance treatment, and sobriety in the other program, yes. All three are the ones, and the mayor of Miami is super conservative economically."

Lucas reiterated, "Get the government out of the way and bring in investors. The Miami Mayor got Dave Rubin of the *'Rubin Report'* there. That's a lot of money! A lot of jobs were emphasized there because it just had economic policies. They would attract that, you know. It's really good! They used the private sector instead of the public sector to fund the stuff," Lucas explained. "Well, it's hard to do that in this town. Private money doesn't come for the homeless. Maybe because the government is in the way."

Enthusiastically, Lucas continued to explain, "If you have low enough regulations and taxes, the money will come. The mayor of Miami reduced the homeless population from 9000 to 630 over the last few years." I asked him if he was going to run for mayor of La Crosse to put into play his ideas. "Ohh, I've had that suggested by people at the cathedral!" Lucas replied. "Maybe I should start with City Council!"

Directing our conversation to another topic, I asked Lucas to talk more about how he was helped through recovery, into a full-time job, and an apartment of his own. "Who helped you when you were at your worst, Lucas?" I asked. "How did you get from the very last day of your worst to the Salvation Army program, to the Cathedral of Saint Joseph the Workman? Were you going to the cathedral while you were living outside?" Lucas began, "Yeah. Sometimes I would hear those super loud bells ringing while I was in Tent City. It's time for mass! I'd get on my bike and go! I just went, yeah!" he said.

I wondered if the individual people at the cathedral helped him. "Yes, they provided the community and the love and stuff. I just gave a speech there last month, a short one about how the love that I once thought could only come from the immediate family came from the cathedral." "That's interesting," I remarked, "because I hear from many unhoused and formerly unsheltered people that they feel devotion and loyalty from and for one another on the street, but not often from the La Crosse community members."

Lucas elaborated on this, "That's what I ask, too. They will steal anything from any of these, from each other, to get their fix. They will! This is exactly what it is. They say that they will help anybody with anything, but they'll steal from anybody. They say that's okay, yeah. It's okay, yeah. But they're lying to themselves. There's no other choice," he said.

"Lucas, you went from that street community choice to church and meetings. Did you feel you were in a community in Tent City to an extent, but you found a better community?" He answered, "Yeah, that community would have to often fight or threaten with weapons, yeah, great community!" Lucas said with a grin.

I asked, "You lived out there, did you say, seven years?" Lucas clarified that he was out on the streets, "for seven years off and on, and then I'd go to Florida for about nine months. I also had apartments for short periods that I screwed up because, apparently, landlords frown upon having ten tweakers over *(note: a tweaker is a person who uses methamphetamines as recreational drugs)*, and a dozen bikes. Landlords don't like that," he said with sarcasm. "I've become reasonable. Landlords don't like little orange caps from the needles everywhere. Yeah, they don't like that for some reason, I don't get that," he said with a grin. "I'm glad you've gotten yourself clean and housed," I told him.

"Without God, I'd be out there right now. Yeah, I'd be in Cameron Park or Burns Park trying to find a little spot to go shoot out my dope somewhere. A public restroom or whatever," Lucas said. When I asked him, "When you say that, Lucas, do you believe that your life is an example of what happens when you turn to God?" "Yeah, people say God doesn't help. But they're mad at God and don't want to take responsibility for where they're at, which means they can't change it. But God does what's happened to me. He made me want it. But they're mad at 'gods,' and they don't want to accept responsibility," Lucas said.

"You're quite young," I pointed out, "and from a family that has had a lot of substance use and abuse, with a mother who died from drug use. To have come out of it successfully is amazing." Lucas nodded, "Most of us are dead. But I'm following my dad's recovery program because he told me for years, and now including as recently as a week ago, that addicts don't stop being addicts. You just have to replace the thing you're addicted to," Lucas shared his dad's wisdom. "So my dad went all in, on work, church, and the Knights of Columbus."

"What else do you want people to know about you, Lucas? Anything else?" He smiled again and said, "Did I mention I'm Catholic!? Oh, and I go to church at Blessed Sacrament on my bike." "What are your dreams," I asked. "What's next for you, Lucas?"

He thought a minute, and said, "I want marriage, children, and to become a Deacon. I did get the cutest girl in the parish to go to lunch with me at Pickerman's today." I joked with him, "So that's why you went to Pickerman's on your day off?" Lucas grinned and said, "I usually go for the soups, but I invited her. I was going to go anyway, but she went with me. She is a nice girl, twenty-five years, thereabouts. I want kids, a wife, and to become a Deacon. If you want to get married, you have to do that first. For some reason, if you become a Deacon first, you can no longer get married. I don't know why. Unless you leave the diaconate, you'd have to get married, be a Deacon, then have kids, all in that order."

When I asked Lucas what his timeline was for these accomplishments, he thoughtfully replied, "I don't know, a year, two years. I'm still working on getting a girlfriend." Asking him if it was the young woman he took to lunch, he laughed and said, "Yeah! But she's out of my league! She took me to lunch because I don't have a car!"

"Any thoughts about your family or getting back in touch with everybody?" I asked him. "It's rough on my mom's side," Lucas said. "There's just some dirty stuff. There were my mom's parents, her aunt, and her uncle, and they all had money. I lived a nice upper-middle-class childhood because of that."

"My mom's older sister cut out my brother and me. It's because my family used drugs. Good excuse, whatever. We were supposed to each get $150,000, both my brother and me after our mom and her parents died. But we got nothing!" Lucas said with feeling. "Our aunt took it all but she has no spouse or kids. I'm her next of kin, but we haven't talked since 2017. She has money! But what's she got, though? No family. Nothing."

I asked if his aunt was close to the Lord or a church community. Lucas was emphatic, "Hell no! She is nobody who acts like they have the Lord." I said, "It sounds like you have no desire to nurture that relationship. What about on your dad's side?" "That's fine, it's good," he said.

"Well, except for my uncle Peter is fighting with my dad about where their mother is going to die. My uncle Peter is number nine of the nine kids. My dad is six of nine. My dad needs a lung transplant so now he's weak. So the youngest one, my uncle, can finally bully one of the older ones, my dad. I heard only my dad's side of it but it's just disgusting. My grandmother wants to die in her house, just like her mom did, and she's ninety-nine and in a home now because of Peter. My uncle thinks he's better than all the other ones because, out of the nine kids, he's the only one who never had a drug or alcohol problem. He's better, I guess, I don't know," Lucas said.

I asked him, "Does your family know that you've changed yourself? If they do, you must feel proud of your changes. I see you have quite a dynamic family. You have some of that, too." Lucas thought about it and then said, "It's because it's so big and we're from New York. If you meet New Yorkers, it's different, and in New Jersey, people are different from the dynamic of La Crosse. A lot louder, more obnoxious, and in your face!" Lucas said.

After answering Lucas's question about when this book might be completed, he said, "I'll hit the campaign trail with the book! I'll promote the book on the campaign trail! We'll both win!" he smiled as he spoke. I assured him that, if any money comes from the book, it will go to Karuna House. "That's a good thing," Lucas said, "but, I hope you get something!" I explained that the book and his interview contribution are to raise awareness in the community. "To help people understand the human aspects of the homeless situation," I said.

Lucas had just completed a podcast about his life. "When that podcast comes out, I wonder if I can get the cathedral and the Diocese of La Crosse to post it to their Facebook page," he pondered. "We'll see. What would your goal be regarding raising homeless awareness inside the church?" I asked. Lucas replied, "Oh, yeah, that would be good. Monsignor Gillis over there appointed me to be the bridge between the parish and the homeless almost two years ago. Now, we have a committee on social concerns doing more. I'm in that, doing a lot more at the warming center. They went from no volunteers two years ago, to thirty with Catholic Charities. The cathedral is the mother church of the diocese," Lucas described.

I suggested that he is "the perfect pick for the liaison to the homeless because you've been there, in the unhoused encampment. Now you're not there. You know a route out of it and you have a plan," I said. Lucas said, "The route out is the sacraments in the Catholic Church. That's a turn-off to some. I'd have to leave that till last. I was just talking with Kevin Decker, the parish mission associate there, who's kind of in charge of the missions. I'm trying to tell him we need to do the recovery stuff. First, you can use AA and NA to lead people to God. But you're not going to get the homeless people to just go right to church and go to God! Not one of them will go to church with me. When I was out there, I think there would be eighty of us in Houska Park and maybe I'd get one or two to go with me, but I'd try."

"Some have talked about Jesus and how they believe. They'll talk about it but they won't walk the talk, and they don't live it. I wasn't doing that well either. I was still going to church but I'd get high after I was done with mass. Well, we've all done that with something. We have to get knocked on the head and have to mature and grow to see who the Lord is. We all get stuck in something, I mean, even if it may not be substance use."

I reminded Lucas that, at the beginning of the interview, "You weren't sure you would be able to answer questions or speak! But you've told me your story!" I told him that I had one more question. "Did you love your mom?" I asked.

"Yes," he said flatly. "When was the last time you spoke with her before she died?" Lucas replied quietly, "A few months before that." I said, "I'm getting the sense that it's pretty painful still." He said, "I don't know, I'm sorry that happened. I pray the rosary for the repose of her soul sometimes. I know that my dad's mom does that every morning. I don't know if she still does. She just is not all there anymore. She's ninety-nine and still more cognitively aware than our current president," Lucas said.

I asked, "Did your family raise you in the Catholic Church?" "Well, all eight of my great-grandparents were Catholic, all four of my grandparents and both my parents." "So all your siblings did. Is everybody still practicing Catholicism?" "No, my brother left to be Muslim while in prison. Pray for him on that. That's rough," Lucas said. "I think only two of the nine kids are still practicing Catholics. The oldest, Uncle Jimmy, my dad." I said, "Well, you have a history with drugs and the Lord. But you've made good choices, Lucas. Thank you for interviewing for this book to raise awareness for unhoused people in La Crosse County."

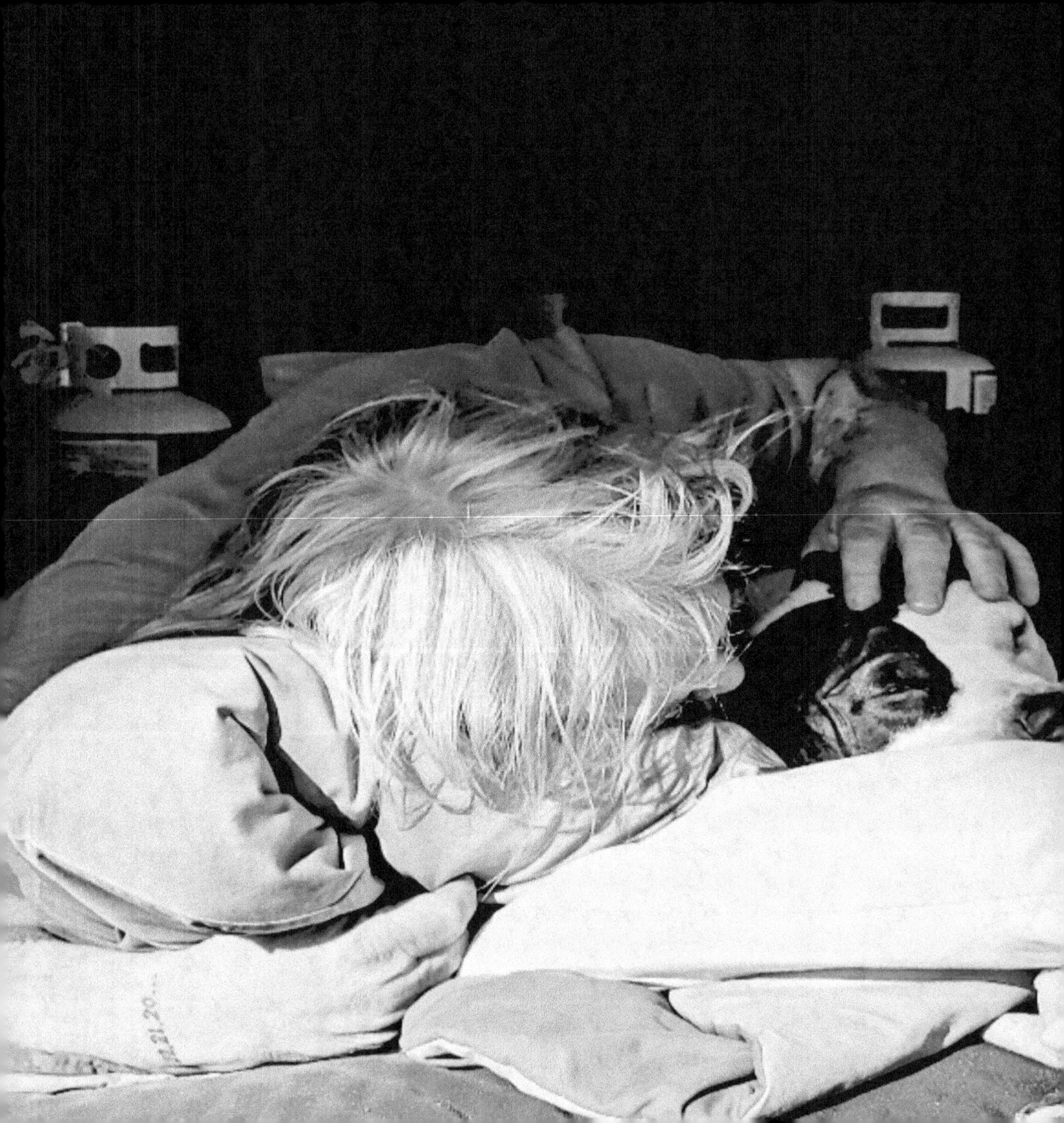

BRAD

BRAD talked with me when I visited Tent City the first few times, with his dog, Zen, nearby. He was a presiding figure among the unsheltered residents and illustrated this by showing me around and introducing me to others. That day was streaming with people stopping by to talk with Brad near a path that came through the encampment near his establishment. His two tents were situated near a sandy beach along the river where he had created a sitting area and firepit. It appeared welcoming and caused several people to stop and talk while I was nearby. Brad made a point of telling people about my book plans and *The Where's Home Project.* He encouraged several to share their stories with me. Some were willing and eager while others were hesitant or uninterested.

Brad told me about a person from the encampment who had died and whose funeral was that day. As people spoke about the death, it was apparent they felt the pain of losing another friend to street life. A woman standing next to me said, "I went to the funeral today. It was a friend of ours." Brad added, "She passed away January 23rd and in her last forty-five minutes of life, I took her pain right here," as he covered his chest with his hands. He said that the friend had a peaceful ending. Then, he began to speak about his life, which he said could be broken into several chronological chapters.

I reminded Brad about a map of the United States that he'd shown me some time ago. A red line was drawn around the country's perimeter on the paper. "You showed me that you had traveled that line," I said. "Yeah, we should break my story down to adolescence, teen, young adult, and then the military," he said. I asked him if joining the military had been his goal or if he had just ended up there. He answered, "I'm going to break the story into chapters. Then, from the military, it's the immediate past afterward."

Brad explained that his mother had met a man named Michael, who became her husband and Brad's biological father. One day, he had a bad morning, but his mom never talked about it. "I didn't understand it until I returned from the war or even why she would never tell me. I carried that all the way, well, almost till I was thirty years old," Brad explained.

"I started life being born right, but before I was a year old, my mom brought the neighbor's car home so we could go to the store. She told me to come, and she drove toward the store. She acted like we were going to the store, but only we didn't. She started but said, *'I can't go back. This is what's happening,'* and drove to my grandfather's house in Stoddard," Brad explained.

"My grandfather called Michael, *'My daughter's home! She's going to stay here!'* He says, *'I'm going to bring the car back up and park it there. Where do you want it?'* So, they agreed upon a midway point, which I think was around The Dells. My grandfather and friend drove up there, parked the car, and left." Then Brad told how, after his grandfather heard the story about what brought his daughter and grandson home, "He went down to Montgomery Ward, bought a rifle, and put it by the inside door to the house. So whatever happened was not very good!" Brad concluded. He talked about his parents' divorce, "It was easy back then because they didn't take anything."

"Then my mom married Jim, and my sister, Dina, was born. She's seventeen months younger than me, so all this happened in that amount of time," Brad said. "He worked delivering beer and city sales. He did a lot of drinking. He came home from work, and my mom was a waitress. They had one more daughter after that, Jamie. She's three years younger than me.

"But Mom worked as a waitress and came home at about 4:00 a.m. Then Jim came home after 4:00 p.m., you know, between 4:00 and 7:00, usually drunk. But the neighbor, a high school kid, would come over and watch us until Dad got home, you know, and fed us, got us ready, whatever. And then you-know-who came home and asked, *'What did you do today? Get in here and bend over!'* because I did something wrong every day, pretty much every day," Brad said.

He described how, when he was a baby, he had allergies, "so I started drinking brandy when I was two years old, every day when he put me to bed. So, as I grew older, I knew what to get for myself!" Brandy! I asked him, "When you got older, say seven or eight?" "No," Brad said, "like a four and five-year-old child!"

Brad continued to tell more of his story. "They were getting mad and throwing me around the house, and stuff like that happened throughout the years. When my mom got tired of it, she kept saying she knew what happened and all that (with her husband). He had a girlfriend! So my youngest sister, Jamie, and I have a half-brother forty-five days younger than her!"

"Do you see your siblings or know of them?" I asked. "Yeah, yeah, well, I mean, yeah," Brad answered. "This woman that he had been with...my mom would get done with work, waitressing, and come home to find her giving us a bath!" Brad continued, "That led to one thing or another. Then I saw my mom get mad and fight with this woman, so I started fighting with this woman. But my mom would stop me because I was fighting with her and hitting her. I hated her from the start and didn't even know it. I didn't even know it, yeah."

"My mom got divorced," Brad said. He was then told that I was the man in the house now. It was when I was nine. *'You've got to take care of our ladies.'* So I did everything that he did to me, I did to them!" He said, "My mom, I hung on her arm so much, yeah, and by the time I was eleven, I was in the system from eleven years old."

When Brad returned home, he would use his mom's car. "I would go see my dad. He was, you know, every other weekend, and two weeks out of the year or something like that, for this visitation. I went twice and, after that, never again!"

"I stayed with my grandparents in Stoddard. Maybe the weekend was commercial fishing with my grandfather, and then winter time was trapping with him," Brad explained. I said, "He sounded like a good and loving man." Brad answered, "Yes, but you did what you were told and didn't do other stuff." He talked fondly of his grandfather and his time in Stoddard along the river. "He was a good man," Brad said quietly.

Brad called his dog, Zen, over, "Good girl. Good girl, good girl." Then he continued, "I spent my summer down there. My dad wanted me to give him a chance when I got older. He made First Sergeant and had me all dressed up. On board and off it, I stood up there after he got his promotion, and I called the company to attention the first time, you know," Brad described proudly.

"Something like that you remember, you know, and feel proud," he said. "These seem like good memories. Are those the kind of memories you have?" I asked. Brad answered, "I have four of them."

"Across the encampment the other day, when you and Bubba were showing me around, I said that they both seemed like supervisors or foremen here in Tent City," I reminded him. "Now you tell me that you were the head of the household, and you called these people to attention at the Armory when you were nine years old!" Brad answered, "I do have guidance qualities, and naturally, yes, because I walk into a situation like this, where people see me as a leader, big time!"

"Yeah, I don't know. I can feel good here," Brad said. We both looked around at the people who had gathered where we were standing. Brad interjected, "Ohh well, that was my dad. Oh, that was one time. Ahh, and then the other time, I got the truck and got everybody at the local bars. So that one time, it's collectively over probably six times during my life. Those were fun days," he said, "because everybody liked my dad. You're watching a kid who doesn't know what's in there, and he says, *'here's a quarter,'* you know, all that stuff—and hanging out at the bar with the guys, both daytime and nighttime." Brad was describing his life growing up with alcohol and spending time with his dad at bars. He said, "That brought more alcohol into his early life."

"But, if you told me someday that I was going to be sober and off alcohol for ten years, I would have just laughed in your face!" he said. "But last year, November 22nd was ten years!" Brad said with pride.

"The hardest part for me wasn't the drinking," he said, "It was the behaviors! You got the same crowd. We'd stick together, arguing, fighting. It's a family thing, you know, whatever." When I suggested that he had instincts about life and his journey, Brad said, "I get that from where I've been. From where I've been. All over."

"Grandpa taught me how to cross the river in the middle of winter!" he said. "I need something to do, you know. I mean, the other day when the ice formed here," Brad pointed toward the river a few yards from where we were standing, "I could read the ice. I just took a walk out there." I wondered if living in his camp along these riverbanks was most familiar and brought Brad a sort of comfort. He told me that his mom was still alive, but his grandparents had passed. We discussed his life story and how he has more years of stories he would like to share.

Thank you, Brad, for contributing this portion of your story to *"Where's Home."*

WHERE'S HOME?

JUNE HART

JUNE HART was eager to share her story. She said she wanted to "help others understand home-lessness and my life situation." She is originally from Tunica, Mississippi, just over the border from Memphis and West Memphis. She spent much of her youth in southeastern Iowa. June was proud to list the states where she has lived: Iowa, Wisconsin, Minnesota, Mississippi, Virginia, Kentucky, Tennessee, North and South Carolina, and Texas. Most of these, she stated, were before she was eighteen.

At age thirteen, June's mother told her to pick a new place for them to live. June closed her eyes and pointed to a map. After her finger touched the Coulee Region area, they came to La Crosse, and June proclaimed it home ever since. A friend called it her *'Ground Zero.'*

June explained what it was like when she first arrived. "I was extremely awkward socially, shy," she said, "and I did not know how to make friends. I did not speak above a whisper and wouldn't look any-body in the eye." June continued to describe that she ultimately made a few friends who wouldn't give up on her.

Eventually, June attended school for criminal justice when she left home to "escape her mother," she said. It wasn't until she was in her thirties that she deliberately pulled away from her mother and brother. "My brother could do no wrong, and I could do no right in my mom's eyes," June said. "When I was fourteen, the neighbors called the cops because my brother pushed me against the wall with his hands around my throat. When my mom got called home from work, she looked at me and told me I shouldn't have antagonized him!" June says matter-of-factly.

"My brother is five years older, so he was nineteen when he did that. He was older and bigger, but everything was my fault, yeah, being blamed, bullied at school, bullied at home, and being shy and quiet. Being abused and harassed, yeah, and then I ended up, I got away from my mother briefly when I was in my twenties."

June told her story in great detail and pain as she explained living with a boyfriend for three years and becoming pregnant. She saw it as a blessing when she said, "We were together for three years, and I had a beautiful daughter out of that relationship. I was in my twenties. The relationship didn't work out, but I was pregnant, and I didn't know what to do or how to handle it or anything. I ended up back with my mother with the baby."

Despite being a problematic and neglectful mother, June's mom was an amazing grandmother, according to June, for which she expressed gratitude. "I couldn't do it without her," she said, "My mom tried to convince me all my life that I couldn't do anything without her. My daughter only lasted, made it until, ohh, ohh," June grieved, "she would be twenty years old this year. But she died at age eight." Continuing to relive her life story through its telling, she explained that her daughter became ill and died. She did not have the energy to have another child or handle losing another one, so she had no intention of ever having more children.

Time passed, and June met someone new, then again became pregnant. "I don't believe in, well, no choice, but I can't..." she trailed off. "Life is too precious," she said as she expressed her values against ending the pregnancy. "I escaped my mother that time," she said. June expressed joy when she described her second daughter's birth two days before the second anniversary of the death of her firstborn girl. "My first girl didn't have anything to do with my second. But the timing is part of their relationship," she smiled. June elaborated on what she believes is a great significance that the two girls connected in timing, if not in living.

June's mother got involved with a man when they moved to La Crosse, so it was this man who was like a father to June, even after her mother had separated from him. Her stepdad was involved in her life and did his best. She described, "He did his best to protect me when I was a teenager and a kid. You know, I moved back home to him in Michigan, my stepdad, and always, but not legally, that's his figure in my life. My stepdad. He put both my girls as important." Time passed, her stepdad died, and June became pregnant with a girl for a third time. She is now four, and her second daughter is nearly ten. Both girls are living with the younger girl's grandmother.

To clarify, June said that she still maintains parental rights, but the grandmother firmly holds the girls away. As June tells this part of her story, it is evident that it is a source of great pain and discouragement. She seemed to gaze into the distance as she talked softly about how creative and beautiful her daughters have become, stating they are the best and worst of both of their parents. "I am happy," June said, "that I had every single one of them."

June continued by explaining her living situation at the time and her addictions. "We had been in a motel room. I did newspaper routes, worked full-time, and cared for the two kids. One of the other people who did newspapers needed a new roommate," she said. "This sounded great because, you know, it was an actual house. It was just her and her boyfriend then, and a three-bedroom house, so I thought it would be good for us." This new living situation ended badly when it became a trap house *(note: a trap house is a house maintained for drug use and dealing)*."

Opening up to talk about her addictions, June said, "I was using Adderall to stay awake and do all the paper routes. I was dating a guy I had met while working at Burger King. He didn't have an addiction but

I was already addicted to Adderall, as I said. But during a special event for my birthday, a friend asked if I wanted some meth. I thought, *'Sure, why not?'* I tried it, you know, once or twice, when I was in my early twenties and this time figured, *'Why not?'* This time I used, I became addicted at age forty-one." She said she is now forty-five and is nearly clean from using drugs.

June is in a four-year relationship with her boyfriend, who is fifteen years younger than June. She believes that he has been like a father figure to her children. He currently struggles with heroin addiction and unemployment but is kind and loving to her girls, a trait of high value to June. Like so many people who battle drug addiction, severe mental health issues, and homelessness, instability in relationships and employment abound and have been ongoing features in June's life as well. She is not timid when describing domestic violence between her boyfriend and herself or spending time incarcerated.

When I asked her about her relationship with her boyfriend's family, she said, "His mom is on my cellphone, but I've never met her. He ended up in ICU when living at Econo because of a blood infection and ended up in a coma. *(Note: Econo Lodge was a shelter for those living unhoused during one winter in La Crosse. It was the first Karuna Inc. living situation.)* My first conversation with his mother was telling her about that." June repeated several times during our conversation, "I've been in survival mode my entire life. I don't know how not to be in survival mode," she said. "I don't know what it would be like if it were different." June's life has been complicated and chaotic from its beginning.

To switch directions, I asked June about her interest in criminal justice and her schooling. "I wanted to help people. I thought it was a good way to do that," she said. "Were you interested in becoming a lawyer?" I asked. "I never wanted to be a lawyer," she said. I wondered what drew her into a technical college's associate degree program in criminal justice, so I asked, "A legal clerk? Police officer? Or Social Worker?" June seemed shy when answering, "I wanted to be a cop," she said, then looked away. "I didn't have any idea before. I had no idea how or what I wanted to do with my life."

Because she was only a semester away from graduating when she quit, I asked about her degree and whether she could salvage the credits toward another program. She replied, "I'm considering returning to school to get the social worker degree at WTC. We talked about being forty-five years old and having a lifetime ahead if she chose to return to school to find a career. She said, "My fiancé would prefer he was the breadwinner, and I would be a stay-at-home mom because it is in his head that this is how it is supposed to work." But she continued to explain that he has not ever held a job, is struggling with addiction, and has similar obstacles that prevent the ideal situation.

June's ability to envision possibility is apparent in most of our discussions, "When it comes to the type of work that I want to do - the kind of social work - I want to work with the homeless," she said. "I want to be the one standing at the top of the hill holding the rope with somebody else climbing up. The thing is, I need to be able to do it. I present well," she reminded me from our earlier discussion. "I'm well-spoken," she said. I told her I saw leadership traits and lived experience in her story." She replied, "I don't know about my strengths in that way. I tend to be quiet and stick to myself often, but I can speak well with people," she said confidently. "I used to look down at people who had addictions," she continued, "because I didn't know what I didn't know. I am not 100%," she declared, "I still do have two addictions."

To explain more about her addictions, June shared, "I have issues with the sciatic nerve in my back, and because I had been honest with my doctors about being an addict, they wouldn't do anything for me. I had been working at the time and doing housekeeping when my sciatic nerve acted up. No one listened to me. Thank you very much. So I went for what I could find on the street. I'm off the Adderall. I'm off the heroin. And I'm off the stuff that got me off heroin. I went to the doctor to get help with my heroin addiction. I don't know that I'll ever be drug-free, right, but I'm okay with that. For one thing, it's honestly made me a better mother," she reasoned.

Talking more about her parenting, June adds about tweaking. *(Note: tweaking is the most dangerous stage of meth use, mainly when use occurs over a long period or in binges. The symptoms of tweaking may not always be apparent to the meth user because they may be using another depressant substance to counteract meth's effects. Tweaking occurs after the symptoms of wakefulness, increased physical activity, decreased appetite, increased respiration, hypothermia, euphoria, irritability, insomnia, confusion, paranoia, and possibly aggression.)*

She explained, "When I was tweaking, I had the patience to sit and do something with my children for hours that I didn't have time or patience to do when I was sober. Isn't that amazing? It is how I was a better mom. It was, you know, the attention to detail and everything like that, yeah. It's also what you need to be a good mom, which people don't seem to get right."

June continued, "I mean, at the worst of my addiction, no, I wasn't a good mom, you know, the best thing that I could do was ask for help, right? People should know. If someone is on Adderall, it is what makes them focus. But it's not just that. If I'm not using it in front of my kids, how does it matter what I do when they go to bed? As long as they're safe, it shouldn't matter," she decided.

I questioned her further, "Is that why the grandma isn't giving them back to you, or does she dislike your boyfriend around them with his drug use?" June explained that the grandmother is protecting the girls from abusive relationships and, "in a way, she also doesn't believe that my boyfriend, Robert, will, well, it's not hers to know, you know. She thinks an abusive relationship can turn out to be abusive toward the kids, so she is protecting them in her way. They've also commented on my relationship, like *'There you go again.'* The thing is, he is fine with giving up the heroin," June presumed. "But he's addicted to both heroin and meth," she conceded.

June said more about her boyfriend's history with drugs and violence. "He was shot up with both when he was four years old. And he has anger issues, and I've had the same anger issues. But I've learned to control my temper. If I can do it, so can he," June resolved. "My friend pointed out that he listens to me in ways that most men don't. He's not a leader. He's a follower, but having said that, he chooses to follow my lead, thank God. For good or bad, at the same time, I will follow him. I don't want to see him behind or in front of me. I don't want that. No, I want to be partners side by side. That's what I keep telling him, and that's what he's working to be good at, for him and good for me, too."

"Also, he displays his best behavior whenever there's a child nearby. He wants to model to her what a good boyfriend and good husband should be. So that's how my daughters' sons or boyfriends should act when they get older," she said but hesitantly slowed and then looked down, as if she herself wondered if this was good logic. "He knows he models the good-boyfriend behavior to my daughter, so that's what she wants to see when she gets older." June reminds me, "He's looking for work for the first time since I've known him. He's never held a job before." June sat silent for a minute as if reflecting on what she had just said.

When I asked June if I could use her real name and picture in this book, she eagerly said, "Yes! I am open and honest about my addiction. I am open and honest about my past. If somebody asks me a question, I'll answer it. I'm fine when I say I'm open and honest."

During our conversation, June teared up occasionally but wept openly when telling portions of her story. The lifelong emotional challenges are ever-present.

Thank you, June, for opening up and sharing your life story with courage.

MARCOS PEREZ

MARCOS PEREZ is fifty-five years old and experiencing homelessness for the first time in his adult life beginning three weeks before this interview. But being unsheltered is not new to him. At age seven, Marcos was left with his eight-year-old brother, Pete, in a Chicago park by his mother. She gave him a note and told him to hand it to the first police officer he saw.

I told him that I was grateful for his willingness to do this interview and share his life story. I said, "I'd like to hear about you, where your life began, your lifetime dreams, and how you became homeless at this later time of life." Marcos told me about his mother. "She left me in a Chicago park when I was seven," he said, then instantly began to weep and was unable to speak.

A few minutes passed before he composed himself. I asked if he wanted to continue and he said, "Yes. I was left with my eight-year-old brother, Pete. Our mother left us," and he began weeping again. "Oh, I haven't talked about this in so long," he shook his head. "I was given a note to give to the first policeman I saw," he said. "We had spent time in that park because we were homeless with our mother. And she knew police officers walked through there." I asked, "What happened next?" He smiled and said, "A police officer came by and I gave him the note."

Subsequently, the officer took the boys to the station. It was arranged that they were placed in their aunt's custody. "She was very bad to us. We stayed there the whole time growing up. My aunt was mentally disturbed. Oh my God, it was very bad!" Marcos put his face in his hands and wept uncontrollably. When he continued to speak, he said, "Nobody checked on us. She treated us terribly. She just took us in for the money. Ohh, it was so many years ago, you know what I mean? But it's stuck right here. It's so dark," he said. "But, what I'm saying is it was so many years ago and all she wanted was the money for us, right? We were wards of the state, is what they called us. So she got that foster care money, yes. I don't know how much but we never saw any of it."

Marcos stopped to think for a moment. Then he said, "My brother, Pete, killed himself in 1988 when he was nineteen. I didn't kill myself, but I tried three times." Marcos sat quietly for a few minutes staring into the room. Then I asked him, "Have you seen your mother since childhood?" He answered, "I was supposed to meet her one time at a Greyhound station when I was nineteen. But I left because I got mad that she left me when I was a kid. I just couldn't do it!" "I understand that totally," I told him, and then asked, "What happened after that, after age nineteen?" Marcos said, "I got married."

Describing his marriage, Marcos explained, "It was a bad thing. All we did was drugs together. It was terrible. It was terrible! She made me do things that I didn't want to do." I asked, "How long did that go on for you, Marcos?" He said, "About six or seven years. I was about twenty-six or twenty-seven. Relationships were bad for me up to that age, except for Pete, my brother. He was the best thing. My brother did everything for me. He did. He really, really did." "That's a heartbreaker," I said, "I'm sure you still miss him today." Marcos replied, "Yeah. I haven't talked about him in a long time but I sure do miss him. It was such a tragic experience to be seven and eight years old and left in a park. So young and then she left me, yeah, she left us. How can anyone do that? How could anyone even think to do that? She left us no explanation, no reason, and nobody else to help," he lamented.

Marcos elaborated on his first experience with homelessness as a young boy. "We were homeless back then and we stayed in hallways. People always kept us down. Ohhh boy, it was bad." He began to cry for several minutes. I asked, "Do you want to talk about what else happened after that?" Marcos began, "I got married a second time and we had a baby. It was a good thing, a great thing! We had my baby named Kaylin who is twenty-five now. She's doing good now. I don't talk to her too much because I'm embarrassed. I'm embarrassed all my life," he said as he continued to talk about the losses in his life.

His father left them a year before his mother abandoned them in a park. His brother died, he reiterated, and his first marriage at nineteen failed after seven years. His embarrassment about life's failures keeps him from his daughter, another loss, he explained. He said, "Before my father left us when I was six and Pete was seven, he handed us a dollar and said, *'Have a nice life.'* Nice, huh? I never saw him again but I heard he passed away."

Marcos discussed other parts of his life. In the past, he was continuously employed doing forklift and warehouse jobs and had a permanent home. Most recently, he was staying with his girlfriend, Tracy, in La Crosse. It was Tracy's employment that kept them housed and maintained their lives together.

According to Marcos, he and Tracy did drugs together every day. Three weeks before I met him, he had an altercation with Tracy's teenage son that resulted in Marcos sustaining a head injury. He grabbed Tracy's arm to get her phone so he could call for help, he explained. "The police arrived and arrested me for grabbing Tracy. I was in jail overnight, and now Tracy and I have a restraining order from the District Attorney." He said, "We cannot see each other or even speak." This is why Marcos is without a home.

Marcos elaborated about the past three weeks since he was forced out of their shared home. "I have been staying at the Salvation Army. But I didn't go there last night because I didn't want to go there. It is so depressing. There's no word to describe it. It is more depressing at the Salvation Army than on the streets," he said. "I don't know. It's hard. Every night, I just have to figure it out. It's getting really hard. This kind of life on the street is new to me except for when I was a kid. I don't know what to do. I just don't!" I asked him, "What are your options other than Salvation Army?"

Marcos said, "The Salvation Army isn't an option. It is too depressing. I can't go back there." "It sounds like your options are very narrow right now. Maybe the best thing is for you to go to the Salvation Army to stay safe at night," I said. "Because I didn't go last night," Marcos said, "I am sure I am kicked out of the Salvation Army shelter. But it's so depressing. It's so depressing," he said as he hung his head and began crying again. Marcos had no other clothes than what he was wearing, no blankets or tent, and no direction where to spend the night. "This homelessness and the streets are new to me. I don't know how to do it," he cried.

I asked Marcos if he was afraid. "Yes!" He replied, "I donated plasma and got $100 on a card, but I gave it to Tracy so she could keep her household." So I suggested, "That might have gotten you a night or two in a motel. Can you ask for your card back from Tracy so you can get shelter?" Instead of answering, he spoke more about the Salvation Army shelter. "It's bad. It's impossible really. Those people talk all night! It's not even humane, no! They give me a place to sleep at night but other than that, it is really scary! They're scary people! Some of the worst, yes, the worst I've ever seen! Ohh my gosh, I've ever seen," he said as he trailed off. "I've been a fighter in the streets for a long time, yeah, but this! It is so scary! It's really scary. I'll just lie down in the grass tonight. I don't know what I'm going to do. I have no idea," he cried.

Marcos switched directions and started talking about his four children. "I have three daughters and one son. My son is in Las Vegas where he manages a store. I tell him, *'Don't be like your father. Don't be like your father!'* He does good though. And I had a grandchild who died on her first day." He raised his arm to show a large tattoo that spelled, *'GIOVANNI.'* He explained, "That is my granddaughter who died. She was born in the bathtub and then she died in a hospital on the same day," Marcos began to weep. He talked about becoming old and said, "I can't imagine getting older. I don't think I'll last that long." Then he smiled. "I love Tracy so much. I promised her I would never leave her! I miss her and love her so much."

Marcos discussed his embarrassment. "I have felt embarrassed all my life. I don't want to ask anyone for help because I am embarrassed. I feel lesser. When I gave the policeman the note our mother gave us, I was just doing what I was told. But in third grade, I had to write a composition on *'What is a Police Officer?'* in fifty words or less. I won the first prize in the city of Chicago and the whole state of Illinois! The police helped me when I was seven so I knew what a police officer was. They helped, you know, but they were down on me, probably because of the way I looked. Now they are down on me because I have tattoos. Head tattoos, on my neck, on my arm. I am discriminated against by how I look," Marcos explained.

There were no answers for Marcos that evening. He was suffering the loss of home, family, his girl-friend, money, and safety. He was also without the drugs he was accustomed to so his discomfort, challenges, and fears were enormous. I left him in the living room of the Karuna House where he had been visiting a friend. The night became stormy and wet so I wondered what happened to Marcos after I left him.

The next day I ran into the Karuna House resident who introduced me to Marcos. I asked if he had any news about Marcos and how he managed through the rainy night. The resident said, "I saw him walking this morning, same clothes, but he was dry. So he must have found shelter from the rain."

I am grateful that Marcos had the courage and willingness to share his traumatic story.

JEFFREY BRANDT

JEFFREY BRANDT shared his story with me in the Karuna House living room. He arrived on an electric scooter he had just purchased from the Mormon Coulee Walmart on the south side. We talked for a minute about how long it took to ride to Grove Street on the near north side so we could meet. Jeffrey said that it took about a half hour. He was pleased that the charge on the scooter lasted the entire way, so he was glad that he decided to buy it over a bicycle which was only a few dollars difference.

He began our conversation by sharing about his work and how he ended up living on the streets. Jeff said, "Not on time enough. I missed out on that. We were City Concrete but I was on the street. Therefore, it's all because of drugs, yeah. It was all because of the drugs. Then this led to legal problems because, not only doing methamphetamines but helping people get it, you know. I was kind of the go-between.

I'm healthy now. I don't use it at all. But I was given less than a thirteen to seventeen percent chance of quitting because I was shooting up a ball a day." Jeff stopped momentarily to explain that a ball of meth is 3.5 grams. "That's a lot!" he said. "I was kind of a functional user. When I started, I had a job. But then I lost my job because of drug use."

I asked Jeffrey to talk about how long he had been clean and what that was like. "I had relapsed two months ago," he said, "but before that, I had relapsed a few months before. But I was good for almost a year! That's strong! I mean, I did it myself. I didn't go to treatment or anything, although I did go to outpatient treatment. I had a little setback a month or so ago, yeah, and felt worse."

Jeffrey explained that he did not begin drugs until ten years ago when he was forty-two years old. "I was engaged to be married and was living with my baby's mama. We were both cocaine addicts. I worked full-time on the island making good money. We were doing it. Selling it, buying it, and using it. Then somebody introduced me to different drugs. I messed up because it kind of replaced living my life. There's a more dangerous addiction to meth."

I asked, "Did you know that before switching drugs?" Jeff answered, "I knew kind of pretty much from research and studying drugs. That's the time I ran into legal problems and received ten months. Basically, not only did the drugs take over my life, but now I have a history that I need to overcome. A past profile big time now," he said. "It's everything. It's incredible really. People used to chase me before I quit, looking for me to help them get some stuff. When I went to the grocery store or gas station, people followed me in their cars to try to get me to help. I mean, I know a lot of people couldn't get it cheap, but they knew that I was an honest guy."

Switching direction, I asked Jeff where he was born and spent his life. He answered, "Here." He indicated he had been here in La Crosse all his life. When asked to talk about his family, he said, "They were terrible. I mean, it could have been much worse. My parents divorced when I was six years old. My mom was, well, in 2019, she would tell you that she was a fantastic mother. If you ask me, I would say she's a great mother by the letter of the law. If she did any less, they would have probably taken us away."

"On a personal level, when I was older, she told me, *'I don't like you, Jeff. You remind me of my failed marriage. You sound and look exactly like your father. Every time I see you and talk to you, you look like your father. You look like my husband! I feel you remind me of my failed marriage! So, you know, I don't like you! You're an ******* just like your father.'* She kept me on until I was sixteen years old."

I asked Jeff if he knew his father at all. "Yeah," Jeff answered. "He moved on to Florida. I talk to my dad every weekend." When I asked if his father was in his life during childhood, Jeff answered that his dad was not at all part of his life until he was eighteen. "He is a good man, yeah. I mean, he's a biker. He left his wife so she treated my brother and me like that. Beyond looking like him and being like him, it isn't such a bad thing. I mean, that's the tough thing with being punished for something you're not even doing. You weren't there for it, so you think your mother's supposed to love you unconditionally."

Jeff kept talking about his life with drugs. "I got caught making drugs on all levels of the business. We made it! We're the first people ever to make it and get caught inside the city limits of La Crosse, Wisconsin. The first people ever, so that's something to go down in the history books!" he stated proudly with a grin. "When I got to jail, I got out two days later because they let me out. My boss said, *'I saw you on the news!'* and then they fired me! I made a little tiny mistake and they just fired me for a mistake that other people do, too. But they still work there!"

I asked, "Where are you working now?" He answered, "I got out of jail and worked at Amazon for ten months. I could not find work, unbelievably, as I was applying everywhere. I've never had a hard time getting a job in my life, but I did then. It's pretty frustrating! Wendy's is the only place that hired me so that's why I'm still there. I'm considering leaving because I've been there for six months. I know six months is the benchmark for other places to hire." "Where would you go from Wendy's?" I asked. Jeff responded, "I'd go to the brewery. So when I work there for six months, I can go to Wabash International for twenty bucks an hour. Then another place after that is twenty-three bucks. I'm trying to climb up and out of this. People were much more difficult than the drugs. All the other people that I associated with to get drugs for or do drugs, don't ever leave. They're relentless! All they care about is getting high. So, if you're trying to quit, they're not good people to know, right?"

Jeff is appropriately proud of getting off drugs and staying clean. "I've accomplished something really big but not much has changed. I was guaranteed and promised by other people that once I become sober, I'll only date sober women! But I haven't dated anybody! Not yet! You know the fall is always faster. I used to be a glass-is-half-full person, and now I'm a glass-is-half-empty negative guy," Jeff stated disappointedly. I asked him, "Even though you defied the percentage of your survival?" "Yes," he said. "But that's just for me. it doesn't matter to anybody else. Half the people don't even believe it! For the people that it should matter to, in fact, like my counselor, it took her like two and a half years to believe me!"

"I also live next door in the dry side of Karuna House where you're supposed to *be* sober! That corroborates other people's opinions of me. Then they tell me that relapse is a part of recovery. Whatever. I think that, at this point in life, you have to take care of yourself and not think about what other people say or do or care or predict. You have to do what you need to do for you. I mean, because who else is going to do it, right? I'm not going to take help. But I would help other people. People come to me for help. I would try to help them. I like helping people and, like I said during my addiction, I even thought I was helping people by getting them the drug. But actually, I wasn't."

Jeff continued, "I thought I was helping, but only in my mind. They built houses instead of putting up tents. I was down at Tent City when I was trying to get better. I was the only one there that had a job and stayed there in a tent. I was trying! There are a lot of people who advocate but there are more who don't. There are a lot of people who don't want to get better. But I did," Jeff said with pride.

I said, "You've made a lot of strides toward that and you have a job. You have the right aspiration to get a better job when you are ready." Jeff beamed, "I want to go back to school. I kind of thought about what to study. Airplane Mechanics in Fox Valley, Wisconsin. I'm fifty-three years old and, even though my best days have passed, I can still make good days. The best is yet to come," Jeff smiled.

"That's right!" I said in support of his plan. "So the best is yet to come. I am happy for you. I feel that you can do this, Jeff." I thank him for his eagerness to tell his story. One day, he will be moving out of Karuna House to Fox Valley for Airplane Mechanics school!

JANA BOLAND-WINDBEIL

JANA BOLAND-WINDBEIL The second part of her story and what happened to Scott begins here. "Someone picked me up so I could get back to the store where I left my phone charger." She hesitated a moment to say, "I'm sorry I'm skipping around so much." Then she continued, "So I got my charger and went back to the hospital, but Scott was gone. He had left the hospital! I was yelling at the receptionist, *'Why would you guys do that!? You know he's going to die! Just let a dying man walk out!?'* There's something wrong about that," Jana said, "I still don't know anything about this. If you're dying and your family isn't there...?"

It's been almost five years since Scott died and Jana still does not know what to make of it all. She was struggling to make sense of this traumatic experience. "The choice should be, if you're dying, there should be something that says you need a second signature. I think this HIPAA thing has changed it too liberally. It is almost uncaring. People are not thinking like that, but I think Scott knew he was dying and he didn't want to die. He told me that he didn't want to die in the hospital."

I asked Jana if she would talk about what Scott wanted, if not to die in the hospital. "He didn't want to die alone," she said. "You were at Stuart's?" I asked. "Yes, I was at Stuart's because I had to find somewhere for Scott to stay. So I told Scott, *'Stay here! I can take care of you!'* I wanted him to wait for me." Jana explained how she needed to find a clean environment so she went to Stuart. He told her that they could stay at his place. "So I went back to the hospital but Scott had left already! He left! Then I started thinking," she said. "I was thinking he doesn't have his walker or his glasses. The night he went to Rat's house, someone there asked to borrow his eyeglasses. He's always so kind that he just let this kid borrow his eyeglasses. Then the kid broke them so Scott couldn't see. He didn't have his walker or his glasses! I didn't know where he was going and he didn't know either, because he didn't even know his directions."

I asked Jana, "How did you ever find Scott after all this?" She answered, "I didn't." She started to motion a diagram in the air with her finger. "So here's the hospital, and Stuart lived through the university over here, on Winnebago. Okay, so it's through the parking lot at the hospital. When I left the hospital, I told Scott I was going to get my charger. *'Stay here. Don't leave. Don't go anywhere!'* But I came back and he was gone!"

"So I started to do a perimeter check. I was thinking, okay, I'm just going to start here, in the middle, and go around. It wasn't dark, but about five or six o'clock. So I ended up at Stuart's. Another friend of ours was in this strip so everybody was over here. I thought Scott might be over there on the right side of the south side of the hospital. But, no, he wasn't, because he couldn't see."

"After he died, I got the police report. Somebody had called 911 and reported a man was stumbling around. They thought he had been drinking but, when they got up to him and figured it out, I read in the report that he had a cardiac arrest right there on the curb at the corner of Division Street. They did CPR and tried to get him breathing again. Then they took him to the hospital."

Previously, Jana called Scott's sister and told her that Scott left. "I explained to her, *'I can't find him. I don't know what to do. We're not married so I don't know what to do. The hospital won't tell me anything. They just said he left! So I'm telling you now and I'm going to start looking for him!'* She lives in Madison and just happened to be coming through La Crosse that night."

Jana told how Scott's sister had five days of food to leave for her and Scott, so she left it at their previous apartment on Fifth Street. *'I'll just zoom in and leave it for you so let me know if you find it,'* Scott's sister told Jana. *'Let me know if you hear from Scott. I'm going to call the hospital.'* Scott's sister said she would call the hospital because, even though she was on his paperwork for emergency contact, they hadn't given her any information. By the time she called, the ambulance had already brought him back and taken him to the Emergency Department."

I asked if the ED admitted Scott and Jana answered, "Yeah, they did. The ambulance picked him up at 7:00 p.m. but, by the time they got back to the hospital and everything was completed, it was 10:29 p.m." Jana described, "But he had passed away. I called the hospital and then went there twice to look for him. His sister called the hospital and was told that he wasn't there. But he was already gone. He had died," Jana said quietly.

"I'm sorry that happened, Jana. What was that like for you?" I asked. "I didn't know he had died until the next night!" she said. "I didn't know any of this until the next day, and then I got the police report." I wondered aloud, "Did they treat you like a spouse after that?" "Never. But I called the police officer who had found him the day before and got the missing person report. I thought I was doing the perimeter looking for him, but I couldn't find him. So I thought, *'Oh, my God, Scott! You must have called somebody. You got it right. You might already be somewhere or you fell over and you're lying on a curb somewhere.'* That's what I said to him. *'God, I have to find him! He's probably lying in a ditch or a curb somewhere.'* Yeah, and he was. He was. But just in a different direction," Jana detailed.

"That night, my friend Jack and I were still walking around until midnight. I didn't know it yet but he had been gone an hour and a half at the time we were walking. I said, *'Oh, his sister said there are some groceries for us at his old place. Let's go over there and get the groceries. At least, maybe he went and got the groceries. Maybe he talked to his sister. That way, I can know if he's been here.'* So, we went, but first we walked. Then, Jack said, *'Hey! Isn't that Scott right there!? Over on that porch with a gray T-shirt?'* I looked up and saw him for just a split second. So I went to cross the road and he was suddenly just gone! It was like he was a light, like a beacon."

Jana started to tell a story about Scott. "I wasn't loving myself anymore. I wasn't loving myself or the people around me. It was winter and there was a homeless man who didn't have a winter coat. Scott said, *'Gilman is cold.'* I said, *'Babe, you're not going to have a coat! You won't have a coat if you give yours away!'* But that's just my upbringing. I never had to worry about others. But that is what I learned from Scott. He said, *'I can get another coat.'* This was the first time I knew that I loved this man. That's what you learn when you open your heart. Because Scott opened his!" I suggested that Scott had left her with a softer heart toward others, "The part you loved about him has worn off on you so, in a way, Scott continues to live on in you. I'd say that's pretty amazing."

Jana reminisced about her times with Scott. She said, "We didn't have a care in the world. We just moved around all day and night getting to know each other. Knowing, loving, and being loved." Many people would be surprised or confused to hear a person with no home, no shelter, no means of making a living or attaining possessions, saying they didn't have a care in the world. But Jana was completely sincere when she expressed this. It was her reality in the life she had with Scott.

But then she said, "I'm so angry! I'm so angry sometimes because I told Scott to let me call an ambulance, but he didn't want me to. I'm so angry I told him not to use that needle! I have gone through this, over and over, this year. If Mason hadn't broken Scott's glasses the night before, or if he had his walker, maybe he could have fallen but he wouldn't have died alone."

I asked Jana, "Is there anything different in your life, besides your grief, since Scott died? Let's talk about your son." She responded, "My son called Scott *'Dad.'* Let's start with Scott number one. When we broke up, we just left my son, Devin. But one amazing thing that came out of those years, just a little over a month after Scott passed away, my granddaughter was born. Jesse's middle name is Scotty. Her name is Jesse Scott, yes. She's got his brown eyes, his brown eyes, but my son has green eyes!"

She was adamant that people understand that Scott was more than his drug addiction, his homelessness, and his disease. "His father was a pastor so he was raised in spirituality. He was writing blogs online about it. He was just like a crusader, you know. He worked with NASA scientists who wrote a paper about plate tectonics. He didn't write the paper but he helped collaborate on it."

Jana changed the subject. "Humans messed up this earth," Jana continued, "and we keep messing up all the time, even doing our best, and God is watching us. He knows everything. We don't know anything."

I asked Jana if she would reiterate how she helped herself, "Can you talk again about how you got where you are now? *(Note: Jana has just signed her third-year lease on a furnished duplex apartment and completed rehab.)* And where did you stay along the way?" She said, "I was, at that point, sleeping down by the river, by Houska. It was before they designated Houska as a campground for the homeless people."

"I was in my camp at the end of November or early December, and I was trying to close my tent. But my zipper broke on the door. So I had these little pins and stuck them all through to keep it together. I had some high heels that I used for tent stakes. I found a big pair of really tall high heels. I didn't have anything to stake my tent down so I used them. It was freezing and the wind was coming off the river. It was a horrible night so I just grabbed everything, put it in a bag that I could carry, and I walked up to the warming center on Third Street."

"I talked to Toni Van Kirk, the woman who ran the place. *'I need help. I can't do this life anymore. I need help.'* So she let me come there during the day when they weren't open. That way, I was away from everybody, and trying to stay clean from drugs. She didn't turn me away because the hours were off or anything. She took care of me and I cleaned the kitchen, did the flooring, and washed all that stuff. I'd help her out in the clothing donation area, whatever they needed, I was there. So for the next year or two, I was housed. That was December 2020 and I got housed in March of 2021." I asked, "What about your drug use during that time."

Jana told me, "I was using and I'm still struggling. But it's been a month. Since Scott died, I still used a little after that. My mom died and then my grandma died two months later. My friend and a bunch of friends from the street died from overdoses. The universe is saying something like, *'You're not dying!'* I got really angry one day when I saw my friend's pictures on Facebook and people making fun of them."

"For a while, I just sat on my phone with these people and argued with them. That's how I got out. I thought that there had to be something else that I could do besides argue with these people who are ignorant and don't give a crap. But they had something to say, so I started thinking. I can't be in the middle of all that down there, all the time near them, because I will use drugs again. But that's what happened! I ended up having slips, a few of them along the way, so I've got to do something from afar. I couldn't let this happen! I went to school to be a paralegal so that's in my blood. So I thought, *'I'm going to fix this! I'm going to find the law. I'm going to find this. I'm going to do something.'*

"At the beginning of the homelessness page *(Humanizing Homelessness Facebook Page started by Jana as its admin),* I was kind of angry. I was yelling at it, you know, the City Council, when I started. I stopped for a second. Wait a minute, there's something more to this. So I started researching everything about homelessness and La Crosse as I could. I started to gather as much information about the laws and ordinances as I could. I wanted to get it in my head. I started using my Facebook page, not for ranting and raving, not for whatever else, but to help the people know their rights and what was being done to them."

"Last summer, we had the Homeless Connect in July. It's where all the local resources come to one place where the homeless people can sign up for what they don't need or don't have or do need.

They got little prizes and things, so I volunteered for that every year. I've been doing that for three years now."

Jana switched topics to Tent City to describe the residents' vulnerability and how they feel about safety and security. She continued, "People like Jen, this person I know, she used to run a church downtown. She was out there picking people up and bringing them to us. The cops were waiting for them to leave their tents. Then they'd go *(into Tent City)* and take their tents and belongings and take them to the landfill. That was last summer. But they did it again this spring at the North River Tent City."

"I want to start having a little task force," Jana said, "so when we know these upcoming encampment sweeps are happening, I want to go down there. I want to stand there and fight! If someone was not there by the time the city came, or even if somebody says, *'No, that's so-and-so's stuff, leave it! They will be coming right back!'* You can't even go to the bathroom or get food or they'll take your stuff! They just want you out!"

"So when I started challenging the cops and the city of La Crosse, and I said, *'You want to know?! This is what I want to do. I challenge you all even if just one of you shows up. I want to make this a real experience for you!'* I said, *'So what we're going to do, we're going to get a tent and find a spot where we think it's okay for us to put up the Tent Camp. We're going to get everything set up. I'm going to teach you how to find food and supplies. You know, dumpster diving!'"*

"That's how they survive out there and how they get their blankets. When Sue was out of hygiene products, clothing, or whatever, that's where we got our stuff. When the college is moving out, we get our stuff." Jana explained how she wants the city personnel, who haul their belongings away, to set up a camp like those in Tent City. Then she'd say to them, *'So, we're going to go and find food and clothing and blankets. We're going to walk and do this, and then when we come back, all your stuff will be gone. You need to know what it feels like to walk away from everything you have to get something to eat or go to the bathroom and wash up, and then you're going to come back and your entire home is gone!'* Then I said, *'I want you to have the feeling that people have when you take all they own.'* I would like to know how they take hearing that! That sounds just like La Crosse. They just look at you. But the only people who are going to fix this are the people who are suffering from it!" Jana explained. "The city is just not going to help!"

I thought about Jana's apartment where she's lived for three years and wondered how it felt to be there where she and her belongings are secure. "What do you feel about having an apartment? Did you find it yourself or did someone provide it?" She was eager to share her story about how she found her home.

"Okay, so they helped me, yeah, and they cover my rent. I'm in 'forever housing' in what is called the *Housing First* program. The basis of the program is to get people into a home whether an apartment, a house, or some other living situation. Get them sheltered!" she said. "And then let's work on their mental health problems, and then let's work on their income issues. Let's work on all this stuff! They are helping in all those ways while looking at your life as a whole. Because they are trying to help people in all these aspects, no way it's not going to work!"

Jana said, "I love the *Housing First* program because it has helped me. It was so funny! When I first got my apartment, the first day my furniture was in there, I was going to have the kids over for dinner. I got some chicken out and just stood there looking around my apartment. *'What do I do? What do I do at a house?'* I wondered. *'I don't know what to do!'* So I just sat down on my couch for a second and looked around at it. It came time to make dinner and I had gotten chicken. But I had to think about what to do next! I had to reteach myself!" Jana laughed.

"How long have you been in your apartment?" I asked. "I just signed my third-year lease!" she glowed with pride. I said, "So you know what to do in a home now, I bet!" Jana spoke up, "Yes and it feels good! There are rules that you have to follow or you could lose it," she said. "I've had a few five-day fix-or-evict notices because I've had friends there who hang out there, you know. There are still a few who I talk to and let them come to shower. That's against the rules to have them come in at all," Jana said with disappointment. I asked, "Not anybody?" "Nobody!" she said, "Because I just got a duplex so someone lives in the front part of the house. She keeps telling on me, but when I get to my door, I have people coming into my backyard. I come from the alley to my door, so they don't even have to deal with her part of the house. She didn't even have to see them!" Jana said.

"What's the step up from here," I questioned. "I don't know. My next thing is that I have no income right now. I have tried getting a job but I have some physical problems now. My back is really bad," she said. "Are you on disability?" I asked. "No, nothing," she said. "Daniela - she's my caseworker for housing. I've been in and out of the doctor's office a lot for the last three years with stomach problems. I had some bleeding, too. Okay, yeah, and then my heart. Once I was having some issues with that but they didn't know what was wrong. Two times something weird happened. I got hot and sweaty, and then my heart was racing," Jana shared.

"I hope you have better care so you can get the help you need," I responded. Jana said, "Right now, I have a really good doctor who helps me out a lot!" she said reassuringly. "So what about money? How do you get by with money? Do you receive any cash money?" I asked after hearing that Jana had been provided with so many other resources. "No, I don't have money, but I have Badger Care and EBT for food." Jana elaborated on the program's complete resources. "Yeah, okay, so I receive medical, housing, and food. But nothing else," she said.

I wondered about the extent of the programmatic provisions, in particular for people who had been on the street for years, have no job history, and are older so are without future Social Security or retirement benefits. "What about disability? I'm wondering because, as people living homeless who are aging out of an ability to survive outdoors, what provisions might be made to help them?' I asked Jana, "If it's okay with you, may I ask how old you are if you don't mind telling me?" "Forty-nine," she said openly. "You'll be retirement age in about sixteen years, but without a work history, what concerns do you have?" I asked. Jana wondered for a moment, and then said, "I guess I don't know how long that I have until then."

I continued, "You will need continued assistance as will many older folks who live outdoors. Something will be needed because, even if you become employed, you'll likely not be able to build a significant work history." In contrast to people with home and employment security, who are concerned about and develop work histories and retirement provisions, the chronically unsheltered populations will need lifelong assistance as they age out of the capacities or resilience to remain outdoors. I pressed the topic with Jana because of its vital importance to the safety and health of many older people who have lived years outdoors or in insecure housing.

"You know," I said, "I have no power or influence, but it seems the Karuna House model addresses this part of the issue as well. They aim for a portion of the cost of living there, a rent of a reasonable amount of any income, and community service as a way of giving back. What is the *Housing First* policy regarding that?" I asked. Jana answered, "They are 30% of my income for rent and then I pay utilities."

As we were winding down our conversation, I asked Jana if she'd like to hear my impression of her as a person. She said yes, she would, but showed a little discomfort. "You have the fortitude, Jana. You show determination and you have a good kind of stubbornness. You're strong to have survived so much distress and challenge, and a great deal of trauma and isolation in your lifetime. As you near fifty years old, you made decisions that resulted in getting you into a home of your own."

"You went from using spiked high heels as tent stakes and little pins to hold a broken zipper on your tent flap, all during a cold December night on the riverfront, to deciding there was only one way out. That was to pick up your stuff and walk for help, which you found because you asked for it. Then you stayed at the warming center, worked on your drug use, and helped out for two years. This proactive initiative you showed was the beginning of your tunneling out."

"Now you don't live outdoors, or survive on leftovers and found objects, but you're uplifted to this, your own home and recovery. You have a degree as a paralegal and you have shown a desire to help those who remain outdoors. You are an influencer. You started the *"Humanizing Homelessness"* Facebook page. You're an activist and an advocate for yourself and for other people who are homeless. You have lived experience and you can speak about it. You are articulate and willing to show the way for others."

"There's a lot that I don't know but there's a lot out there that I still do know," Jana confirmed. "When I was out there, I never really had any problems with anybody. They all liked me so that helps out a little bit, too, I think. I have a certain amount of trust in them and they have the same for you. Losing Scott was painful but I didn't die. It happened to Scott. But as a person, I survived." I assured her, "Yes, you did. It is a huge responsibility to stay clean from drugs, maintain your home, and share the story with others as a way of giving hope and guidance. You have created something significant for the homeless community."

Much gratitude to Jana for sharing her story so others can have hope. Things can change with the help of the community and each one stepping out of the status quo. Jana did it on the cold winter night when she gathered her belongings and walked from Houska Park to the Third Street Warming Center. She refused to let her previous life keep her down!

TENT CITY IMAGES

River North 2024

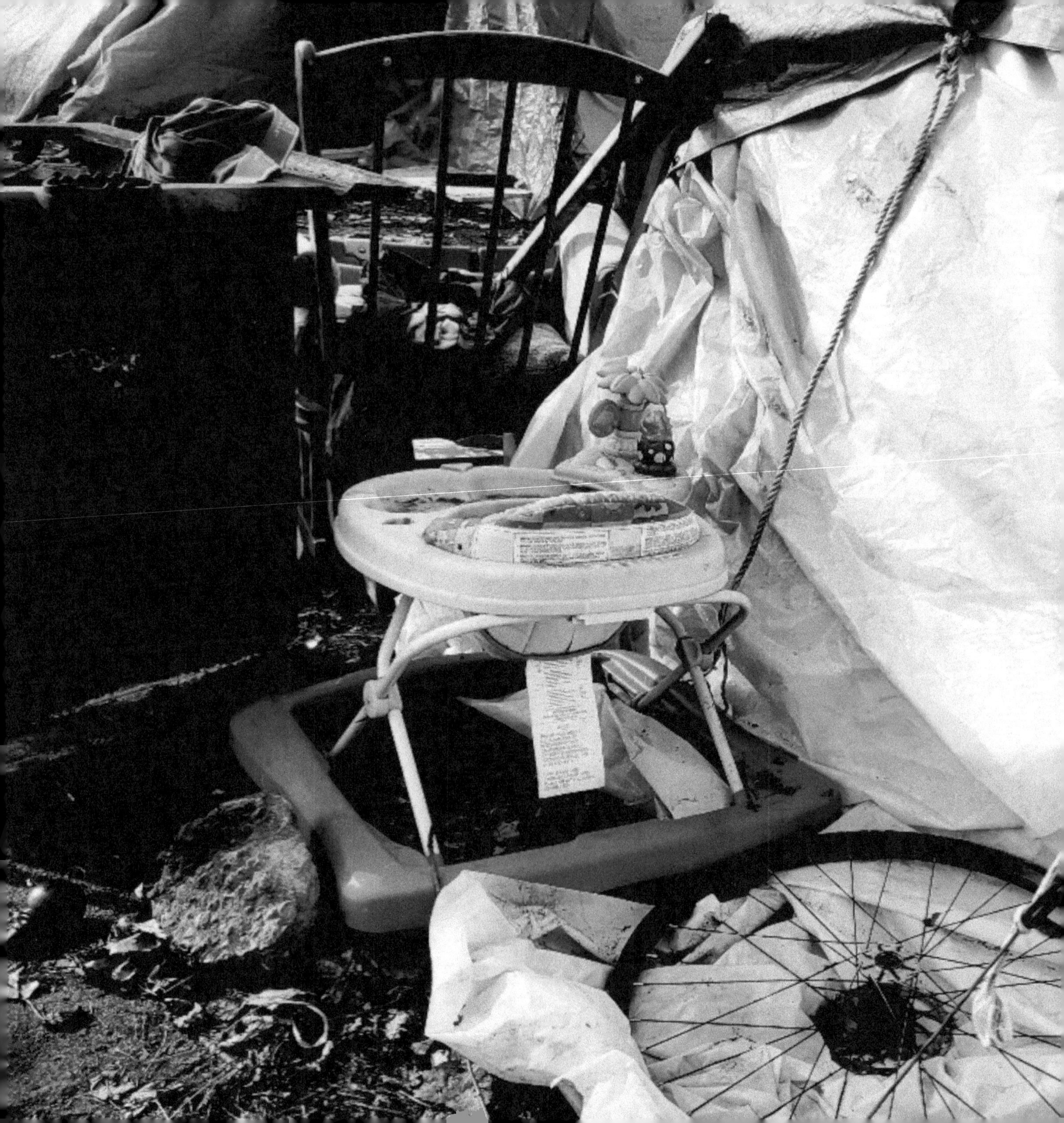

Karuna Inc.
Finding a life worth living

KARUNA HOUSE

JULIE McDERMID continued to share about the Econo Lodge experience as it came to a close, and share about the beginning of the Karuna House Project. She said, "You've got people who are severely addicted. We weren't going to stop that from happening. Was it going to be the thing that was going to get someone kicked out? No, addiction is not going to get you kicked out of shelter. Is it going to prompt a conversation about recovery? Sure," she said frankly. "I think people get all caught up about saying there was drug trafficking going on. But, no. Drug trafficking usually means a certain amount of drugs are passing through. But we're talking about people who are severely addicted. If there was drug dealing happening on site, certainly, if any of our clients were dealing..." she trailed, "but they were making so much money, they could go rent an apartment of their own! But they were trading used clothing, hygiene items, and bicycle parts. We're not talking about drug trafficking," Julie said with clarity.

"We've talked about who the dealers are and that is a different story *(than trafficking)*. They also do it for survival. The people were dealing from the inside and we knew who they were. They even have their own addictions to feed so they might be making only a little bit of cash here and there. They're certainly making out better than the clients that they're selling to..." Julie slowed as she made her point. I asked, "Is this more like playground trading for the benefit of those on the playground? It's not to become rich and have power over anyone, right?" "These are not folks that are making money hand over fist. That's not the kind of dealing that happens. It's not the kind of dealing that generally draws that much attention from the police."

Julie discussed that, "Sometimes there were frequent complaints about statistics that stated there were over a hundred police calls to Econo Lodge in a month. I questioned, *'Was there a massive trafficking operation, and were the police just walking past this massive drug operation?'* No, it's not realistic. Although those are great to talk about. They make great stories and great statistics if someone is trying to tell a story or to prove their own point, or if people don't like the homeless and don't want to spend money on them. But that's not actually what was happening," Julie explained.

"It was much more complex than that. At the same time, people didn't want to hear about parts of it. Did we house as many people as we wanted? Did we have some complete recovery treatment in a five-and-a-half-month period? Yes, seventeen individuals, which is unprecedented!"

"Some of the positives and successes were just accepting people where they were, you know, and not kicking them out because they got caught using or they got caught with drugs on them. We did search the rooms every day. We did go in and check everyone's rooms every day and confiscate what we found, but that wasn't going to get anyone kicked out," Julie said assuredly. "That just meant that we were going to talk with the individual. I think that is what led to a lot of people feeling supported and not judged. They had hope. Hope for being able to stay and hope for a home," Julie said.

I asked Julie to explain, "What did you confiscate? If they needed their drug, did you take the drugs from them?" Julie answered, "Yes, we confiscated drugs, even if they needed the drug. We take the same policy or the same approach that Catholic Charities Warming Center does, which is that it's still illegal. We can't have it or it's endangering the whole project by allowing that. If someone goes out and uses, then comes back under the influence, we were okay with them being on the premises as long as they could control their behavior but we would confiscate the drugs, if they had them. I think most people understood that, although it didn't always stop them. So that was the practice that we had there at Econo Lodge."

"It was, in a way, a bit of a trial. Figuring out how to manage that was a difficult thing to do. I will never do harm reduction on a scale that large again," Julie stated. "That's very hard to manage because there are so many under the influence and the behaviors can be really hard to manage in a large group setting. But I think it's certainly worth the effort because, I think, that's where people feel supported and where they can grow."

I reflected on what Julie just explained, "It's very interesting. I didn't think about this before you were talking about it. But usually, we scale up after starting small. But, with Karuna House, you are scaling down from the Econo Lodge project. In trying to make that work, you're using the same philosophy and practices, I suppose, and trying to make them work scaled smaller. What is that like for you to figure out how to scale something down that was so huge? Karuna House is ten people versus the hundred and sixteen who were housed at Econo Lodge." Julie thought about it a minute and then spoke. "Managing the Karuna space is so small. It's not that it's a piece of cake but it's just different."

"In our original proposal, I think we projected as many as forty or forty-five people living on-site, with maybe six to eight overflow shelter beds in the Econo Lodge building. That was what we envisioned long term as far as creating living space services. But it changed when we agreed to work with the city. They wanted us to shelter as many as needed to get everybody off the streets. It was cold and during COVID, too. It was much bigger and not our target population," Julie explained. "It was for anybody homeless. But our target population is the chronically homeless and, in particular, people who have been through supportive housing before. Of the hundred and sixteen people sheltered at Econo, anywhere from a third or half of them would have been considered chronically homeless."

This perspective was new and interesting to me so I asked Julie, "What makes this distinction between the groups of those unsheltered and the chronically homeless?" Julie was thoughtful in her response. "I'm not sure how we landed on that group," she said. "It is a good question. There are a couple of ways that tend to be the demographic."

"Some folks were able to use the hotel as a safe landing spot as they worked to transition out to their own housing. This group of people only needed transitional housing. It was almost too much supervision and oversight for them so, as a result, they wanted more freedom. But we saw the chronically homeless group do very well in the hotel setting. The other thing that I learned, working for the collaborative and with our data, was that we have quite a few people who go through existing programs more than once. It is not because those programs aren't great, but more because they're just not the right ones for that group." Julie explained this complex dynamic and then continued.

"Once someone fails in a supported housing program, most of the time they go back to living on the street because that is what they know. They then also go back on our community housing list and usually go straight to the top of that because of their lengthy history of homelessness and high barriers to staying housed. The number of barriers they face puts them back at the top of the list and they go back through the programs over and over again. It's just the way that HUD *(U.S. Department of Housing and Urban Development)* directs us to choose clients," Julie said.

Julie glanced at me and said, "You interviewed one of these individuals, I think, who cycled through four different CouleeCap apartments. Another person who you interviewed has been in program housing, and then unhoused, back and forth. This cycle happens for these individuals because they don't have the support or supervision that is required for their success. They're not ready to be in unstaffed or individual housing but not because they're little kids! They just need more support."

Julie continued, "I think one of the factors is that they become lonely when in individual housing situations. We have a resident here *(at Karuna House)*, who you didn't interview, but who was in a housing program and doing pretty well. He struggles with addiction and gets very lonely. While in individual housing programs, he let his friends in because he was lonely. Then they all were using and got piled up in his apartment and, eventually, he was evicted and homeless again. One of the things that he loves here at Karuna is that we do have staff on-site twenty-four hours and, although he's never had to say to his friends, *'You need to leave now,'* the very thought of staff being here helps him feel a little stronger."

"Some of our current residents need more help managing better health care. They need people on-site to help them remember to take medications or keep appointments. They need that daily encouragement which is not something they can get from our scattered site programs," Julie finished. "I see that they may never get past that need in their life," I remarked. Julie responded, "Someone may just need that intensive support for a short time before they can move on, but not every individual has the same need level." I realized that this is why Julie and her group had selected forty as the number of homeless individuals for the original Econo program. It was approximately the population of those chronically homeless.

Breaking down some other details regarding the Karuna House model, Julie explained, "It's a twenty-four-hour budget that supports this housing program," she said. "It's intensive support that is associated with a large price tag. It is a permanent supportive housing program, for the most part, but the majority of people in the homeless population don't need this type of service. For this group of people, it is needed. When they are given individual apartments without support, it clogs the system. If they are placed in these programs where they're not going to be successful, they are tying up resources, staff, and apartments for two or three years, by cycling through like that. It is a two or three-year investment that a program opens which could have gone to somebody else who could have moved through and been successful without all the support, and who might even grow out of housing to something on their own."

"Some chronically homeless folks do well in scattered-site supported housing but others do not. When they become homeless again, they end up on our housing list another time and, because of their background, they quickly rise to the top yet again. This means they're going to get selected repeatedly and all these other people who have more middling barriers, never get selected. But these super high-barrier folks keep going through the programs, rising to the top of the list, clogging the flow of the programs."

As I began to understand the intricacies of these circumstances, I realized that I had interviewed someone who expressed frustration with this exact dynamic. I said, "A woman I spoke with had continually tried to get into the housing system and grumbled about those who were wasting their opportunities by being placed in nice housing, as she saw it. She told me, *'They can't stay, but I can sustain housing on my own. I just need help getting into it. I'm qualified for that!'* she said. "Yes," Julie agreed, "They're people who will complain and even get angry because they've watched this group of individuals receive multiple housing opportunities. Then they get kicked out of it but get right back in. There was a person who was given a place and then destroyed their last apartment. They screwed it all up by using drugs and becoming unable to sustain the opportunity."

Julie continued, "People who need housing and witness this, think that these people don't care about the opportunity they've been given. But they do care! They're just not supported in the right way they need to be successful. Many people in the system and those on the outside, think there is a flaw in the system. I have talked about it a lot with all of our founders. We understand how it works, I think, and that it's complicated. A lot of people don't understand how our housing systems work generally so I am, for the most part, almost speaking another language when I talk to the general population." I told

Julie, "For me, gradually, as you have iterated this to me, I am understanding it. I am certain more and more people will grasp some knowledge of it, too, as it is talked about more in our

La Crosse area community and in the *"Where's Home"* book where you have been very clear."

Going back to the Econo Lodge project, Julie said, "Out of one hundred thirty-eight unduplicated clients who we served at the Econo Lodge, twenty-six had been in some sort of supported housing program before entry into our program. That was just our shelter for those five and a half months. There were twenty-six who had been through programming and then ended up homeless again. The goal of those programs is not to recycle, but to give these people a home. They can grow if they can stay, yes, so that's a failure in the programming. It is not because the programs are not good, but it is just the way the programs are built. It's a scattered site model that is done all over the United States and the State of Wisconsin. They are not the only programs that do it this way, nor is it some fatal flaw. It is just that a piece is missing."

I asked Julie, "Is it similar to chronic illness? If that piece is in place, it makes the other ones more efficient and work better?" Julie answered, "Yes, exactly. That is where we landed! Number one, we saw the Econo Lodge model working for that group of people. Number two, it was great that we had a group of staff that loved working with that population. Many of the same individual staff members returned to the various Econo Lodge projects, many who liked working with the population."

"We knew from the data that it had the potential to have a broader impact than just the people that we have housed. If we can take this group off of the prioritization list, some of these other people who are further down the list could be super successful in the scattered-site types of programs. If we can move those people up into those openings, we might make the whole system more efficient!" I interjected, "It's in the public schools. There are ways built into the system that give rise to different ability levels, hopefully without the clogging that you have described with housing situations. The same thing happens in various systems where the flow continues to repeat itself or the clogging repeats. It is like gravity in the sense that we don't have to make it work, but it just works on its own if we place the right pieces in the right order."

"This is also what was seen from the Econo situation. It took apart these details and revealed them to show these things and how they could work," I reflected. "So that was the Econo Lodge project. Talk about when it ended," I said to Julie. "We essentially spent five and a half months just trying to make things work," she responded. "It was sort of chaos the whole way through as we managed this group of people and tried this new harm reduction approach. I appreciate the city, the county, and the Police Department being patient with us. They knew that was the approach we were taking and they were alright with that. We were encouraged by the city. They wanted to see a very low-barrier shelter but, when it ended and the funding was completed, we had to close the project down. We had just one day when everyone just dispersed. It was at the end of April because the lease agreement ended and the weather was better for folks to go outside." I asked, "So you emptied the building and just gave it back? It was just done?"

"Yes," Julie said. "We ended up transferring all the people out. Some went back to Houska Park. A lot of other people went to shelters and housing. We tried to get people into the Salvation Army or another shelter program if they didn't have housing or treatment or something else lined up. But a lot of people went back to Houska. We went back to the drawing board because, at that point, we'd gotten hit with some great media and some not-so-great — the not-so-great media was one of the biggest factors in starting small. We had to repair our reputation. Some of the clients spoke on our behalf and talked about all the great things that they had been able to achieve. We had worked with New Horizons Center and Outreach *(for domestic violence)* and were able to get some women away from their abusers and into other shelter situations. I think the city and county both were generally happy with the job we had done or, at least, knew that we had done the best that we could with what we had."

I asked Julie to talk about what happened next that brought us to the current Karuna Housing. "We looked for buildings because we'd tossed around the idea of scaling way back and starting small. We wanted to prove our good name again and show that it works, you know, on a smaller scale. Because of the cost of requiring twenty-four-hour staffing, we couldn't scale back to a single house rental for three, four, or even five individuals to make it even remotely cost-effective. We would need to do at least eight to ten individuals to justify the staffing costs and make it balance out because it's prohibitively expensive for a smaller number of people. We began the search for *The Unicorn*, as we called it."

"The perfect building would have the right number of rooms and the right amount of amenities. This is where Sister Karen was very much our hero. She was going on every realtor website and apartment search. Very quickly, she found out about places and called. She told them what we wanted to do and they were immediately against the idea. *'You want to put homeless people in right now!?'* and she wouldn't hear back from them. We spent the time writing a new business plan and searching for property throughout the summer."

"We followed a lot of our former clients from Econo Lodge so we tried to provide support services through that summer. We had two staff held over from the hotel plus myself. We were able to keep our staff paid but we tried to be super frugal. We focused all of our energy on trying to find the property, The Unicorn. It was Sister Karen who found what is now our current Karuna House in La Crosse. It was occupied but the student leases were up at the end of the summer. The owners and management said that they'd like to give this a try. They loved the concept, they said."

"It is a rooming house model for which we had to get licensing because of zoning codes. What is nice about it is that, as far as construction planning for the future goes, we're saving money because we are not putting in a kitchen and bathroom with every single bedroom. It is a saving not only in money but in construction and space. The bedrooms in this particular building are adequate living space and so we like the model. We want to make sure that people have adequate and dignified space to live in, especially for people who may be living in it for the rest of their lives. What we're finding though is that we're seeing some success with the six-bedroom model."

Julie explains further what she is thinking, "If we are to eventually construct our own building, I'd like to see us do different size units. It is not always easy to find six people who are going to mesh well in a situation, especially if people are going to be living here permanently. There are absolutely some people who I believe would do better in an efficiency situation or a one-bedroom. For now, this is our two-year pilot housing that gives us the time to work on the needs and see what works, and what doesn't work, and to make sure that, in two years, it will be time to move into our own building. We want to be certain that this is physically the right space and that we have our programming down so that it works for the population we are targeting."

I asked Julie how she felt things were going thus far. "I have signed our lease for the second year. Our leases started in August and September. The two different sides of the building are on offset leases due to prior tenant situations. So our leases expire a month apart. Earlier this year, I went ahead and signed a second-year lease so we're good here until early Fall of 2025. So far, everything is going very well with our landlord and they've had no complaints. I think, even if we had this for a third year, depending upon our construction and timeline, I think we could do that. The sooner we get into our own building and expand to capacity, the better because it is much more cost-efficient," Julie stated.

I said, "So you're already talking about *when* you get a building, not *if* you get your own building. Is this how you hope it will go, or do you know it will go like this?" Julie grinned and answered, "Well, that is hopeful. I mean, that was the same thinking that drove us into one hundred sixteen people at Econo." "Is that why, with this building, it was not *if* you find the right building, but *when* you find the building?" I asked. Julie grinned and said, "Yeah." "Where does that come from, that kind of thinking?" I questioned her. She said, "I don't even know. I think it's just a very stubborn thing about me." I was puzzled because it did not exactly match up with a mental health history of immobilizing depression. "I've got to question it because it doesn't go with the mental health history you have described, which is more of a hopeless and powerless way of life." Julie responded by saying, "This is like, *'I'm gonna do it!'* I think that's true as an example but I think there's also a piece that is a sort of..." Julie hesitated and then said, "I almost hesitate to tell people what is at the root of it because it might scare them a little bit. But I almost feel like there's a little bit of it that's just, *'if I'm not doing what I want to do, if I'm not moving it forward, then why live at all?'* I expressed my surprise by saying, "It's an all-or-nothing? Yeah? Or are you trying to stay ahead of depression that can pull you back down?" Julie paused and then thoughtfully said, "I pull myself out of depression every other day, but it's a separate thing. I think it's, for some reason, to me, it feels like the driver. That I don't want to go back there and there's nothing to lose. There's nothing to lose. I suppose that we could lose or the project could fall apart. But, if we don't take steps forward, it's going to do that," she completed. I stated, "That's a real hopeful motivator. Could it be that it's like climbing up a wall? The alternative to keep climbing up is to drop to the ground and perish." Julie responded, "It's not futile but it's making things come alive. It's something that I learned a little bit, too, while working with the collaborative and from Erin Healy. *'Do something, don't get stuck in planning – take action. Move something.'"*

Deviating for a moment, Julie said, "There were six residents who had been at Econo Lodge in the winter of 21-22 and who died the following winter when they didn't have enough shelter. It was heartbreaking. Just heartbreaking!" Julie revealed. "I believe this is the other driver for me. It's life or death essentially, yeah, so just keep moving." Julie continued, "We're trying to turn the tide of the community, get funding, and just help, it has to be intentional."

"Every year on December 21st, we do the Homeless Persons' Memorial which is done nationally. December 21st was chosen because it is the longest night of the year that people are outside. It's cold and the longest night that they have to survive out there. We do a memorial and honor people who have passed away during the year, either while they were actively homeless or who were formerly homeless. Those numbers always get media attention. That's very hard for a lot of people in the community. Our community is fairly evenly divided. Some just don't want to deal with it and believe that the homeless population isn't helping itself. Some don't pay attention to the numbers and then there is half the population that wants to help but, at the same time, doesn't know how to help. I think it's difficult for almost everybody to look at and know that we're failing."

"In part, it's a lack of understanding and awareness," I said. "A woman's body was found up on Hendrickson's Trail on the north side. It was publicized but there is little if no follow-up about what happened, who she was, and so forth. The news seems to get lost. Perhaps it's difficult for a community person to follow. Other deaths, for military troops for instance, are identified and reported, but when it is an unsheltered person, the statistics are not broadcast and the people are not named or honored in a timely way. There are areas of this entire issue that disappear or are only murmured that keep us uninformed, from seeing the truth. To be frank, I never heard about six individuals found dead in La Crosse over any winter. This is only one way that unsheltered people are disenfranchised," I said, "and marginalized. It is demoralizing. We should be past the days of potter's fields and leaving individuals unidentified or without naming their family."

"You're right," Julie agreed. "It's overwhelming for people to think about. Even fellow providers who work in the field become overwhelmed. It is difficult when you know this person or that person who you knew or worked with, and they've passed away before your eyes. I think that, oftentimes, people tend to explain it away by saying the person didn't die of homelessness, but of addiction they brought on themselves. But it's not the drugs or the addiction. It is that they didn't have a place to live or somebody talking to them about recovery or looking out for them. They were sticking the needle in their arm at the Econo Lodge and they didn't die," Julie said.

"The deaths are a harsh reality. For a while, I simply fell apart. I just couldn't focus. I felt that it was hopeless to continue, to write that business plan, because I was so mired in it while, at the same time for me, it is a particularly strong driver. I might wonder for a little while and then come back here. It just made me a little different than how other people work but I think that definitely it is a motivator," Julie revealed.

"Despite how it brings you down and challenges your emotional stability, you are strong and have a tolerance for vulnerability to systemic and human dysfunction. You have a strong ability to do this work and have a lot of emotions about it," I told Julie. She said, "But the people who live outside have to have a high tolerance to be able to live out there and be so vulnerable." I responded, "Maybe it's difficult for the general population to become this vulnerable and be open to a population that is always so vulnerable. Julie, you are not averse to allowing yourself to see vulnerable people every day in your work. You have already been vulnerable in your own life. But it isn't this job that makes you vulnerable but you're open to the vulnerability that comes with it."

Julie said, "I guess it is what I'm trying to see. Vulnerability, I think, frightens many people into complacency and confusion about what to do. We do well but, if people would just get vulnerable, it could help us figure out what to do."

"We all worked alongside each other as we learned how the system worked and we advocated for different changes. We attempted to do a homeless Bill of Rights here at one time and then withdrew it after receiving a cease-and-desist order from the Mayor's office. We've tried things and failed for one reason or another. Then we tried again. Each of us has struggled personally throughout and then, somehow, ended up at it again," Julie concluded.

Thank you, Julie, for sharing this vital story of the unsheltered citizens of La Crosse County. Karuna House, your work, and the efforts of those with you are essential to finding the housing solution for all. You are so appreciated!

KARUNA MISSION

KARUNA HOUSE is a mission to build a stronger community by providing supportive housing models that empower people experiencing homelessness to cultivate resilience, elevate personal dignity, and find a life worth living.

The inaugural Karuna House Supportive Housing Pilot Project offers a supportive housing model that does not currently exist in La Crosse. It combines the physical living situation and support needed to sustainably house chronically homeless individuals who have intense needs.

WHAT IT LOOKS LIKE

- co-living style apartments with rent assistance
- 24-hour intensive, peer-based support on-site plus professional case management and care co-ordination
- Community connection, integration, and engagement through group recreational activities and required community service

KARUNA SERVICES

SERVICES ONSITE

- Comprehensive needs assessment and care planning
- Available private space onsite for medical, mental health, and substance use professionals to provide service at the residence
- Exploration and planning for career, employment, entrepreneurial, and education goals
- Independent living skills training
- Support for learning about healthy hobbies, local support groups, and other activities that foster personal growth and a sense of well-being
- Housing navigation and transition support for when residents are ready to move on

KARUNA COLLABORATION

THE PROBLEM
Chronic homelessness in La Crosse is growing at an alarming rate.

- More than half of homeless individuals and families in La Crosse need intensive support to address complex medical, mental health, and substance use needs.
- An increasing number of individuals and families have been unable to maintain their housing and are returning to homelessness even after participating in existing supportive housing programs.
- The costs to both the community and the individual or family experiencing homelessness are too high a price to pay.

COLLABORATION
Karuna knows that residents who are connected to a variety of supports will be more likely to sustain their housing and thrive in the community. Staff work to engage partner organizations that can help each resident achieve their personal goals for housing, employment, education, spiritual development, and recreation.

JOIN OUR EFFORTS

THE KARUNA TEAM

Karuna Inc. is made up of a team of individuals with combined decades of experience working with individuals and families experiencing homelessness, housing instability, mental health crises, and substance use disorders. Our staff has accomplished backgrounds in Peer Support, Recovery Coaching, Community Health Work, case Management, Independent Living Skills training, and Pastoral Care.

INVITATION TO JOIN EFFORTS AND SPONSOR A RESIDENT

While residents are required to contribute a rent payment, most are not able to afford the full monthly cost. Additionally, Karuna does not charge residents for supportive services. You can join our efforts and support our residents by contributing financially to the Karuna Supportive Housing Pilot Project. **The cost of rent for one resident is $4,000 per year ($335 per month).**

This information is published in the Karuna Inc. *"Finding a Life Worth Living"* brochure. To receive more information or copies of this flyer, contact Karuna's staff:

· Karuna House Office Phone 608-360-6430 | Karuna House Cell Phone 608-317-8936
· Emails: juliem@karunahousing.org | aleshas@karunahousing.org

Visit our webpage to learn more about Karuna Inc., our pilot project, and how to donate: www.karunahousing.org

BOBBI RATHERT

VIEWS FROM THE FRONTLINE

Views from the Frontline

- *Julie McDermid*
- *Alesha Schandelmeier*
- *Jonathan Walters*
- *Barb Pollack*
- *Mark Schimpf*

JULIE MCDERMID

JULIE McDERMID is the Executive Director of Karuna Inc. She agreed to sit with me one afternoon at the public library to tell her story. "I think it is probably interesting to know that I'm not from La Crosse," she began. "I was not born and raised here but have been here the last twenty years."

"I was born in New Jersey. I have a theory that everybody passes through New Jersey at some point," she smiled. "We lived in Maryland when I was very young, but then moved to the suburbs of Chicago," she explained. Since my history has roots in Chicago, too, I asked Julie where she lived in that area. We talked a bit about the area and the common boundaries we shared. "We lived in the north suburbs of Chicago, Buffalo Grove," she said. "I went to Stevenson High School because I was on that side of Lake Cook Road. We had kids from Lincolnshire, Highland Park, and Deerfield." Julie told me about her college choices once she graduated from Stevenson.

"I was slated to go to Loyola University. It was the only school I was interested in attending to study archaeology. I got early acceptance to Loyola and it was super close to home. But it didn't work out because of the cost. My financial assistance would not cover it all so my parents suggested I live at home and commute. My interest then turned to Quincy College which was offering me almost a full ride." Then Julie laughed and said, "I would have rather been on a farm in the middle of nowhere than continue living at home! So I went to Quincy."

"I don't know how many times I changed my major. One day it was history and the next day it was chemistry and then philosophy. Then it was political science," Julie smiled. "I had a teacher who was a lot like that, too. He was a political science teacher who then went to the same college where he taught. He wanted to do a physics degree, so he understood about changing interests like that. We took a math class together, so we'd go to math class, but a couple of hours later, I'd be in his class! He said to me, *'You have an interest in a lot of different things but you haven't figured out what it is you want to do yet.'*"

Out of college, I lived overseas in Uganda for three years. I worked with Habitat for Humanity International so that's where I first started to understand the importance of housing. It wasn't until years later that I began to understand what a crucial piece the Habitat experience was to me. I loved Habitat."

Julie explained more about Habitat for Humanity and how it affected her. "It has a very spiritual philosophy about housing as our foundation. If you ever read about Millard Fuller, Habitat, and Jimmy Carter, it's interesting. Habitat for Humanity was started with Millard Fuller who was a lawyer in New York City. He was tired of the rat race and wanted to do something closer to his Christian values. So he moved his entire family to a Christian community in Georgia called Koinonia Farm that was led by Clarence Jordan." I asked Julie if this was where the connection with Jimmy Carter began. She responded, "Yes, it's not far from where Jimmy Carter was living. I never really thought to look into that history, but it's interesting." *(Note: visit www.fullercenter.org for more information about Millard Fuller's philosophy, writings, and videos.)*

"The communal farm still exists. The Fullers lived there for a while and then felt they wanted to go out in the world. I don't think Millard Fuller was interested in living his life out in a Christian commune so they ended up moving from Georgia after five years to Zaire. This is where they founded Habitat for Humanity and started building houses. The Fullers eventually moved back to Georgia to really build the organization and then Jimmy Carter got involved. It's an ecumenical organization that is rooted in this theology of the hammer. It is really wonderful," Julie thoughtfully said. "I always wanted to work overseas but I wasn't sure what I wanted to do. So, when I was out of college, I applied to Habitat for Humanity International."

When I returned home, I didn't know what to do with myself. I always struggled with my mental health as a kid and in college. But overseas, I loved it." When I asked Julie why she returned to the States, she explained that her parents had divorced while she was away and her grandmother, who she was very close to, was quite ill. "I was very close to her," Julie said, "so I came home."

"I just wasn't sure exactly what I wanted to do with myself." I asked, "Did you come home when the program ended or did you just decide to return?" Julie answered, "Habitat used to do three-year terms. They offered a second term but, with my parents divorcing and my family situation at home being kind of funky, I knew I needed to be home, at least for a little bit."

"So I came home and just got a job in retail so that I'd be doing something. I was living with my dad and brother in the Chicago area, but eventually kind of ran away with a guy who I had dated for a while. We moved to New Hampshire. It's interesting," Julie explained. "They talk about culture shock. I think I had a harder time coming back from Uganda than I did going to Uganda initially. It was really hard to try to get reassimilated back into suburban city living. When this guy said he was going to New Hampshire and was going to rehab a cabin in the woods, I thought of the White Mountains and said, *'Let's go!'* So off we went!"

'Well, that didn't pan out," Julie said, her eyes sparkling. "The trip itself was a good thing. It was interesting so I definitely wouldn't trade the experience. But the relationship thing was not so good. I drove across the country in a broken-down car and then I came back across the country in the same broken-down car but with a different boy!" Julie laughed.

"We went to Caledonia, Minnesota, which was his home area and lived there for a while. Then we broke up after a couple of years even though we were going to be married," Julie explained. "We broke up just before that happened," she said, and then added, "which was a good thing." I asked, "Did you stay in Caledonia after that?" "Yes, I stayed for a while," Julie said, "And then I moved to La Crosse."

Julie shifted the subject to her mental health challenges. "I started to get bad when I was in Caledonia. I figured it just came to a point where I wasn't moving around anymore and wasn't sure what I was going to do. I seemed to have lost myself in all these relationships and I was trying to figure things out. *'I'm in an area that I don't know very well. I don't have a family or anything around,'* I was thinking. So I ended up in La Crosse."

"I had attempted suicide a couple of times, pretty seriously," Julie revealed. "The first time, I was in Caledonia. I was institutionalized at Mendota and then sent home because they said that I was too high functioning," Julie grinned, rolled her eyes, and then continued. "They sent me home to Caledonia. But my parents came and packed my things. They moved me to La Crosse because they felt uncomfortable with me in Caledonia. Because I wasn't willing to go back home with them, I moved to La Crosse."

"I tried to make it work for a little while but eventually had to apply for Social Security. I got Social Security benefits so, for about the next ten to twelve years, I did nothing. I just circled the drain," Julie said. I then asked, "For home, did you have an apartment, or a house? What was your shelter during that time?" To explain, Julie said, "Yes, I had an apartment. I've never been homeless but I was almost evicted once. Mostly because I was so depressed, I wasn't paying my rent."

"Then my dad passed away. I was very, very close to my dad," she said. "It was very sudden and about two weeks after his sixty-fifth birthday. He passed away from a massive heart attack overnight. My mental health changed after that." Julie elaborated on her circumstances. "I think I started being on Social Security benefits about 2003 or 2004 and my dad died in 2005. I was doing therapy and trying to go back to work here and there. I got connected to Independent Living Resources *(ILR)*. Through all that, I tried to go back to work, but something would take me down every time."

"The last time that I attempted *(suicide)* was 2011 and it was very serious," Julie explained. "I had just started a therapy program called DBT, Dialectical Behavior Therapy, so I just signed on to do that. But I attempted and they were even a little worried that I wasn't going to be cognitively capable of doing the DBT anymore. It was a little bit of a journey back. I think it was enough of a scare that I realized I was either going to have to do something radically different to get better, or I was going to end up in a nursing home somewhere."

"My therapist was great and was the one who gave us the tagline for Karuna House. *'Finding Your Own Life Worth Living.'* I don't think I realized, in the hospital, how serious it was. When I got out and met with her, I remember she asked certain very basic things. I just answered and then looked at her like, *'What?'* She was asking me things to check my cognitive state! She said to me, *'We were really worried. You know, Julie, I think you need to figure out what it is, what you're moving towards. You can do all the therapy in the world but, if you don't have a goal or something that's making your life worth living, I don't think any of this is going to make you grow.'* She told me that people live for all kinds of reasons. They live for a relationship that they're in or for their job. Then she said to me, *'I don't know if you struggle with that.'* I had heard that before," Julie remembered. "From my college professor in Quincy when he told me I had an interest in a lot of things but hadn't figured out what it was yet. So it wasn't surprising to me when my therapist said that. Yet it took a while but I sort of threw myself into that therapy and I got a whole lot better. I still don't know that I knew exactly what I wanted but I knew I didn't want to be where I had been."

"I had been connected to ILR for help and trying to go back to work. I was still on Social Security benefits so went through the Department of Workforce Development. They hooked me up there to receive help writing a resume and get some internships. Eventually, I got a job there but left it. At ILR, the Executive Director, Kathy Noble Iverson, who is now retired, said she liked what she saw in me. She said, *'I get it that you can't work right now, but why don't you join our Board of Directors? I think you have something important to say.'* So I did that for a while," Julie concluded.

"When I was finally able to truly go back to work after I started therapy in 2011, I had worked through it for about a year and a half," Julie explained, "and Kathy asked if it was time to apply for that job again. So I did. I went back to work for ILR for the second time as an Independent Living Specialist in housing. It just clicked. It was going back to my roots with Habitat for Humanity and understanding what a crucial piece it was for me. I loved Habitat and its very spiritual connection to housing as our foundation."

Julie shared more about her application to Habitat for Humanity after college. Her boss at Habitat told her, *'I didn't know, Julie, that you have a very glass-half-full sort of thing.'* That's a lot of what you need when you go overseas. You kind of let it fill you up and go with the flow. Otherwise, that culture change can be really difficult."

"I was in a group of ten going through orientation at the time. I was the youngest and the only single female. There were three single guys and three families with kids, and couples. They thought, *'What is she doing here? She has no skills!'* But, I'm the only one that lasted all three years!" Julie said with pride. Her boss told her that it wasn't her resume or education. *'It was your glass-half-full spirit!'* It was about learning how the community works, and being willing to let that experience fill you up," Julie continued, "and being able to share the basic structure of Habitat because it looks different at every affiliate around the world."

"I'm stubborn," Julie shifted the subject to talk about her fortitude. "I have to remind myself about this. I remember, in third or fourth grade, I took piano lessons. My parents had a teacher who came to the house to give me the lessons. I'd come home from school and be so tired that, instead of going outside to play with other kids, I put on my nightgown and got in bed. I remember my mom waking me up when my piano teacher arrived on lesson days at 4:00 p.m. Even my mom was surprised I was in bed but I was always struggling with depression. Just like out of college, there was a lot of crazy in my house."

Julie continued to share about her early life. "I had two alcoholic parents who were very well-to-do in the community, but alcoholic. There was a lot of fighting. It was miserable and I just wanted to get away. I knew I wanted to do something different and wanted to see the world. But I remember being terrified the entire time, but going anyway," she said.

I asked about her family structure and whether she had siblings. "I have a brother who is very different from me. Even though my whole family is very liberal and democratic, my brother is a very conservative Republican." Julie explained that, since her dad died, they have not been connected. "It was one of the only things tying us together."

"You certainly have gotten in touch with yourself," I commented. Julie said, "I always feel that I have this weird way of looking at things in my head. I feel like I'm also attached to stuff. I can be a little bit of a hoarder and always have dragged stuff with me wherever I go. I took a lot of stuff to Uganda. I brought a lot of stuff back from Uganda," she smiled.

"Every time I moved, I took a lot of stuff but I also left a lot of stuff. I feel that I always have this feeling in my head that I'm leaving some part of me behind everywhere I go. I felt the more I traveled around, the more I lost myself. It was this thing where I had to get out of my house to go out in the world and figure out who I was, but when I was out there, it was so overwhelming. My mental health wasn't good, so it was also really difficult. I slowly started to crumble more and more."

"When my dad died it just kind of…" Julie then trailed off. "Pulled the rug out?" I asked. "Yeah. So that's a lot of years. I say that's important because I think, you know, my brother and my mom are still alive. My mom knows how I feel. She's pretty mentally ill herself and has a lot of problems. I couldn't stay tethered to that. The more I got better with my mental health, the more I had to be away from that. I think my brother resented it because I wouldn't come home to help take care of her. I wasn't spending a lot of time at home so he was stuck with that a lot. Frankly, my brother, at the time that I stopped speaking to him, was pretty deep in his alcoholism."

I asked Julie about her parents' drinking and whether they ever stopped. She said, "My mom stopped drinking. My parents stopped drinking during the divorce so that they could each go to court. So that each could say they were the sober ones. That's the way my home and my parents' whole marriage was, one big competition throughout. My mom became obsessed with other things like her weight. She dropped a huge amount of weight, to the point that the doctors encouraged her not to lose any more! She becomes one unhealthy coping skill to the next." We laughed together at the common adage that people often switch addictions instead of recovering.

After I asked if her mom was living on her own, Julie said, "To my knowledge, she's still living alone. I don't know that she's necessarily able to, but she is stubborn. It's where I get my stubborn streak, from her." I commented that Julie has used her stubbornness for good, to get well, and to help others.

"I just think all that experience taught me, you know, is that family could be more than just the people I was directly related to by blood. I had to build that for myself. Home is more than a physical structure. I had to build it for myself. Identity was really important and *'finding that life worth living,'* figuring out what we are doing on this planet, and having some sense of purpose was important, too. I also feel I could understand some of the experiences that people are going through with their mental health or addiction."

"I've steered clear of substance use like alcohol and drugs, although I did experiment in college like everybody, so I feel can understand it. Going back to work for ILR as an Independent Living Specialist in housing, I worked a lot with the homeless population. I was technically working for ILR with anybody who had a disability and a housing issue. So it could be somebody who is looking to move from an institution out into the community, or moving around in the community, or looking to find more independence. But more often than not, it was the homeless population. I just found that I could relate to that group. That's what I loved about working for ILR. We were encouraged to use our lived experience to share with others to help them on their journey."

I observed, "So a perfect match. Even though you didn't experience actual homelessness, it sounds like you didn't have a home growing up. You lived in a house, but it wasn't a safe home for you. It didn't help you discover who you were as a person."

"Ideally, as parents, we're supposed to help children do that work to strengthen their identities and, in a perfect world, it's done in the homes by the parent figures, in whatever configuration. In that sense, you were without home and those comforts for your entire formative years," I considered.

"It's awesome how, in your ILR position, you were able to unravel that connection and combine your life experience with ways that help others find their identity as best as they can," I said.

"I think working at ILR, I gained a huge amount of knowledge about all of our housing systems from subsidized housing, income-based, the different supported housing programs for homelessness, and to shelters," Julie explained. "That's where I was able to work with all of this other frontline staff and these other agencies."

"In 2016, Erin Healy came to La Crosse from New York. Sandy Brekke and Gundersen sponsored her visit to La Crosse to evaluate how all of our agencies and systems work together around homelessness. It was also meant to give the community a report on how we might be able to do it better. Erin had worked for Community Solutions and was now her own consultant."

"While she was here, she sat with a number of us who worked on housing issues. We all sat around a table talking about housing and related issues. I remember saying something to her about having copies of all of the subsidized housing and income-based housing projects and the applications on file. Erin said, *'You do?'* We were the only two subsidized housing nerds in the room," Julie laughed. "Erin said, *'I would love to see those!'* We hit it off," Julie remembered fondly. "Erin worked with the community about ending veteran homelessness. We had that initiative back in 2016 and I was chosen from ILR to be part of one of the collaborative teams to do that work. I was pretty excited about it."

"After doing that, the whole town was jazzed about it. The community, with financial backing from La Crosse Community Foundation and the United Way, said, *'We need a project manager to continue leading us to do this, with Erin Healey mentoring.'* When that job became available, I applied and got the position. So I went to work for the Collaborative," Julie explained.

I asked Julie if she would explain Erin Healey's assessment and how things went forward after she returned to New York. Julie agreed and said, "Erin assessed that the

La Crosse community has a lot of resources that work together on a lot of things. But here's where we can do it better. Erin brought us the idea of doing sprints where, for a hundred days, we focus on a certain population, like veterans. Then later, we did chronic homelessness, and then that was followed by doing families. Erin brought a lot of those strategies to us. Everything that Pathways Home is doing is built on Community Solution strategies. The By-Name list and understanding data, all that kind of good stuff started with Erin's action here. She's a pretty cool person."

"I wish you would be able to interview her, but she's not here," Julie remarked. I nodded, "Maybe next time, we can go deeper with an interview if Erin comes back." Julie continued, "I worked for the Collaborative for a couple of years and, of course, we had the pandemic outbreak at the beginning of 2020. I was with the Collaborative through almost the end of 2020. I left in December of 2020, so I was with them for about three and a half years. I was with them throughout that first year of the pandemic and helped to coordinate the additional shelter that we provided."

Julie began to explain in depth how the COVID-19 outbreak pressed on the homelessness efforts in La Crosse. "It was especially bad at the outset of it when everything shut down and people couldn't be outside. There was nowhere they could go. So Catholic Charities worked with a local school to use their gymnasium to expand their warming center because the Salvation Army was at maximum capacity. We knew we needed to be able to have enough space to shelter everyone who wanted it. So we moved the warming shelter to a gymnasium for a while. Then, things started to ease up."

"I remember driving around the streets and there was nobody. You know, it was like something out of a science fiction movie. Nobody was moving but we had people sheltered for quite a while. People had to stay because, if they left, we didn't have a way to quarantine or bring them again to stay in there. They had to stay in, or they could go on the school property and couldn't interact with anybody."

"As the weather started to warm up in about May, we couldn't keep people. They had lived outside and they wanted to go outside. Over the summer, some people wanted to get into the Salvation Army but, because they had left the shelter, they weren't allowed back in. They were fearful that there would be a COVID-19 outbreak in the shelter. So I worked on a small project with the county where we rented some hotel rooms at the Econo Lodge."

"We were supposed to be quarantining people for fourteen days and then transferring them to the Salvation Army. We were able to get some of the people straight out to housing and others were able to transfer." Julie elaborated on the strenuous process of providing sufficient health and shelter services for those unhoused in the county. "Towards the end of that summer, in August, it was apparent that the homeless population of La Crosse needed more assistance to keep them safe. Various ideas and efforts were launched, some were more effective than others, but still, this population was increasingly vulnerable." After a meeting was held to discuss options, Julie shared an idea that linked current services at Econo and the necessary services needed for the unsheltered population.

Julie said, "I don't have a community health background but it seemed to me we had to be practical to keep the people safe. So I said, *'If the city and county have the COVID Relief Act funds, we could think about offering to rent out the hotel.'* The first time around, it may have seemed too complicated so we went ahead with the school gymnasium. So I just said, *'We've got a dozen rooms right now so why not rent out the entire hotel and kill two birds with one stone? We can house all these people who desperately need shelter, and we can test them for COVID as they come in. We'd be able to separate in triage fashion those who were positive, negative, and who needed medical care.'"* At that point, I was asked, *'How fast do you think we could do it?'"*

"I gave the details some thought and said, *'We have a pretty good relationship with the hotel owners. We can keep a pretty tight rein on things.'* I was asked if we could have it up and running within a week. I gave it some thought and, considering satisfying staffing needs and other practical details, I thought we could do it," Julie smiled with confidence. She was right. "We filled that entire hotel with human beings and this is where they spent September and October," Julie said.

"The entire county or world had hopes COVID would lift by early winter, at the most. So, locally, it was thought that the Salvation Army and Catholic Charities would open and take up where they left off early that year when COVID-19 began." But, according to Julie, "Toward the end of October, we were beginning just then to see the population increase. So many people were coming into homelessness. They were losing their jobs. A lot of those folks who became homeless were frontline workers at restaurants and retail businesses. They didn't have work during COVID and, when business didn't pick up right away, there were still all those COVID restrictions about how many people could be in a space. Those people didn't have jobs so they lost their homes."

Julie continued to elaborate on the pressures of COVID-19 on sheltering the homeless population. "We were seeing the population go up for the first time in years. I was an advocate of keeping the hotel. We had it open and got it running. I said, *'Let's keep it going and keep everybody sheltered so we don't lose any people.'* I felt like there was more money coming down the pike, so to speak, through not just the COVID Relief Act but the American Rescue Plan Act."

"I believed we could spend it on shelter because it was better spent there to coordinate our efforts and focus on getting people housed at the hotel. Although not everyone at various agencies agreed with me,

I believed it was the best option to consider. Because we were seeing an influx of dollars like we'd never seen before, and an increase in this very vulnerable chronically homeless population..." Julie trailed. Of course, there were challenges and problems with the operation, as Julie described, but it was a difficult time with something that had never been dealt with before.

Julie and her staff set up much of the hotel structure to address families, individuals, those who were well, and others who were sick. She managed the staffing, food, housekeeping, sanitation, and COVID-19. In the end, it was effective if not truly successful. "That's an amazing thing that you are describing, Julie, and so many La Crosse residents didn't know it was going on while they were isolated in their homes," I marveled.

Meanwhile, I asked if Julie would explain more about Shelter Development, something she had mentioned in her discussion. "Yes," she said, "it is the organization that is behind The Exchange, which is a project of Shelter Development. They are continuing to work on their family program, which is awesome. I took the job there and they wanted me to work with them because they thought I was going to be able to help them develop that," Julie explained. "I think I started in March or April of 2021."

"Not long after I started at Shelter Development, I shared that my colleagues and I were talking and had dreamed up a project that included purchasing the Econo Lodge. What if we, as a group of people and the community, were able to somehow buy the Econo Lodge? We could convert the rooms into small apartments, maybe join two rooms to make very small efficiency types of space. We could have apartments for the chronically homeless on the upper level, maybe some on the lower level, and maybe we'd have some rooms for overflow shelter. We would have space that would become offices for services onsite and we'd have a big community kitchen. We have all these dreams, you know."

I asked, "How many rooms are in the Econo Lodge?" Julie answered, "There are sixty-six. We had these thoughts about it and we kept talking. I created a little rubric, like a logic model, and we started to write a plan. Shelter Development agreed we could arrange a meeting with some funders and representatives from the city and county at the Econo Lodge. We wanted to tell them the idea," Julie said. "I told them, *'I don't have the background or experience to do this, but we're going to need a business plan.'* There were a couple of people in the room who were quite interested."

"Not long after, the city suggested that it buy the Econo Lodge and provide the money to operate as a shelter until the population went down enough. At that time the number of people camping in Houska Park was growing by the day and the city was concerned they would not have enough shelter for everyone when the campground had to close at the end of October. Then they could give *'first right of refusal'* to turn the building into whatever we wanted after that. The question was posed, *'What do you need for us to do that?'* They said, *'Write a plan that we can put before the City Council'.* Then literally, the city negotiated a selling price with the owners of the Econo Lodge."

Julie went on, "At the time, I was now working two part-time jobs - one for Shelter Development, who we hoped to develop the Econo Lodge project idea with, and one with BLACK *(Black Leaders Acquiring*

Collective Knowledge) to start up a youth homeless shelter in the area. I was writing the plan and taking it to the City Council. Everybody was in favor of it so that was what we were going to do. We were hoping to solve the winter shelter problem and trying to get us off the ground."

"So as this moved forward, I continued to work with Shelter Development, hoping they would want to be the organization to do the Econo Lodge Project. It wasn't until their Board said they weren't ready for this large of a project and we checked with other organizations, like St. Clare Health Mission who declined because housing was not a part of their mission, that we went back to the City and said, *'Sorry, we don't have anybody who will do it. No organization will do it.'* City staff member, Jay Odegaard, suggested we could create our own organization. We hadn't thought it would be possible but he gave us the encouragement to move forward and do it. We incorporated in September as Karuna Inc."

Julie discussed how much else was considered and exchanged, between her and the City, and with other people and agencies. In the end, even though Julie's group had incorporated as Karuna Inc., had a Board of Directors, submitted a plan, and had several interested investors, the cost of the project was still prohibitive. There was pressure against it so it did not pass the City Council.

Other ideas floated, including renting the Econo Lodge with an agreement to put a percentage toward future ownership; or simply renting the hotel due to the sizeable unsheltered population scattered in town and Houska Park with winter nearing. The City initiated a Request for Proposals (RFP) so the process became more competitive.

"Other agencies put a plan together to manage the Econo Lodge through the winter. The RFP was due at the end of October and the city staff were going to make the decision which of two groups received it. It was about October and the City meeting was around November 12th," Julie said. "City Council was meeting to approve the funding and then November 15th was the day it was to open."

Julie shared the personal side of the experience. "I was exhausted and depressed. I just couldn't believe it. Here we were, on the precipice of doing this dream project. Then it just got destroyed. We had just written a thirty-seven-page business plan and then, they were asking us to write an RFP. We talked about it and decided that we wouldn't write our response to the RFP. We would say, *'You have our business plan. That's our response and we think our business plan addresses everything that you want in your RFP.'* We thought our plan addressed everything they wanted, plus more. The city staff person who led the contract hire told the City Council, *'We only received one response and it was from the group of agencies. So that's who we're going with.'*"

In the end, there was concern that the group that was awarded the contract was not going to be ready in time to provide shelter starting November 15th. The Council voted to approve the funding to be used to provide shelter and encouraged City staff to go back and review both proposals.

"So I went home," Julie said. "I was thinking it was still uncertain. But then I received a call from Jay Odegard who said, *'Are you ready? You got the contract!'* I was flabbergasted and terrified! This had to be a quick turnover because the deadline was still the same! The deadline was still the same!" Julie repeated. That was one of the questions, *'Can you open on that next Monday?'* It was in three days, that Monday!" Julie said excitedly. "We got the answer on Friday and on Monday, we had to open the doors! Here we had stopped all of our planning and hiring because we didn't get the contract."

Julie told more of the story. "I reached out to Mark and said, *'You're not going to believe it! We're doing this! Unless you think we shouldn't be doing this,'* I added. But we did it! We reached out to everybody because we have such a great group of people! When we did it back in 2020, we had to do it. We had to get it up and running in less than a week because it was a public health emergency. So it was about just finding those dedicated individuals who would be willing to do it. So we called everybody and said, *'Are you willing to come and be there?!'*"

"We had a process. We had the mobile Med Team. The City took school buses and loaded them at Houska Park. They only loaded fifteen people per bus to take them to Econo Lodge. They closed off the streets to Isle La Plume so other people, besides the Houska Park Tent Encampment, would not attempt to get involved. They loaded people and their belongings on the buses. The mobile Med Team was doing COVID testing, giving vaccines, and taking medical histories with the people as they drove to Econo Lodge. They got off the buses at the Econo Lodge where we had a brief orientation in the lobby for each group of fifteen people. Once they had done that and their intake paperwork, they proceeded to the registration desk and got their room assignments."

Julie continued this amazing story. "We were supposed to shelter no more than sixty people. That was what we were estimating. We were going to be short shelter beds but we ended up sheltering 116 people in eleven hours!" I was in disbelief and said, "Transported, through orientation, registration, intake paperwork, and into bed, in eleven hours!?" Julie was smiling and said, "Yes, and into bed for three days to quarantine! Houska Park was empty!" Julie almost shouted. "And Houska Park was empty! This was 2021 and COVID ended in 2022," she reminded me. "Originally, the City was renting the Econo Lodge for November through March and they ended up extending it through April," Julie said. I said, "So you were there all winter, managing people and keeping them well!" "Yes," she said, "And we received new people, coming and going. We did take in some new clients and we also discharged people. We tried not to discharge people but throughout the whole of that five and a half months, we served 138 unduplicated clients."

"We did some family motel vouchers for people. From there, we did get some people into housing." I asked if people were placed in more permanent housing all through the winter or if were they mostly kept safe and warm at Econo. "Mostly kept safe and warm," Julie replied. "There were a lot of things going on and we struggled with maintaining community health workers. They were supposed to be sort of our primary case managers but that didn't work out as hoped."

"I ended up working with some of my staff to do case management with people. But we were struggling because, at that point, we were already in a housing crisis because of COVID and our numbers were huge. Nobody moves in the winter anyway, and nobody was moving during COVID. There were eviction moratoriums so people weren't relocating. So there wasn't a lot of housing available."

"People grew on each other's nerves and they wanted to change roommates. It worked out kind of nicely because changing rooms also helped people keep their rooms clean. After all, they wouldn't want to move into a dirty room," Julie grinned. She continued to talk about the struggles and challenges they had on a daily and nightly basis. Included were mental health issues, addiction issues, infighting and arguing, and minding the rules. Police were called when things were out of hand but, even then, the number of calls to police involving the homeless community was much less than in pre-Econo and pre-COVID days.

Julie explained, "I think they said that there were between 100 to 120 calls a month to the police from the Econo Lodge, and largely it was the same few people who we were calling about. There were a couple of people who had such severe mental health issues and coupled with substance use issues, we still had many fewer calls than ordinary. We just dealt with things through the whole winter," Julie said. Econo was successful during these difficult times and many people were kept safe, warm, and healthy through that winter.

Julie continued to talk about the positives of the Econo project. "We got a whole bunch of people housed, not as many as we had hoped, but we sent seventeen people to treatment. Seventeen is unprecedented!" she said. "I think that was because we had a lot of staff who had lived experience and shared that. There were some great stories there."

Sharing one very poignant story, Julie began, "We had a husband and wife. He had done prison time for drug sales and gone to treatment three times in that five and a half months. He kept going, coming back, going, coming back. The last time, it finally stuck! The wife went. She was more thoughtful about it. She didn't go until towards the end of the hotel but she ended up going to a different place than her husband. They went to separate treatment centers. She went to Madison and she chose not to get back together with him immediately. When she was still in treatment in Madison when we did a presentation to the City Council, she attended virtually to tell the council about her experience and how supported she felt."

"During the City Council meeting, I'm going to get all teary-eyed," Julie warned me, "but during that presentation, she had been in treatment and was waiting to hear about a woman's halfway house opening in Madison. She wanted to stay in Madison where she went to treatment, but she was kind of running out of time for Medicaid to continue to pay for her bed and treatment. So she was thinking she would have to come back to La Crosse."

"Well, the night that we did the presentation to the council and she attended virtually, she told the council how important the project had been to her. She said, *I want to tell you, I just found out today that I got a spot!* and we were all crying and so happy for her! You know, ohhh! and she and her husband have since gotten back together and moved back to La Crosse when they were clean. They have now been clean for over a year!" Julie said with a huge smile.

I said, "Wow, what a story! I was going to ask you about that. About this type of success story. I'm sure there are all kinds of configurations of people getting better, struggling, but still trying." Julie agreed, "Yeah, so it was rough but I think we probably sent back to Houska Park, out of 138 people, I think 55 or 60 were sent back out." I asked, "Would that be to the River North Tent Encampment?" "No," Julie said, "to Houska Park. So they went to Houska then for that summer. The first summer, Houska Park was kind of under the radar. The City was just kind of diverting people there and it got really big. At the end of that summer, we did the Econo Lodge project. Then the second Houska Park summer, it was approved by the state to be an official campground. They had all been given the tents. I think it was about 55 or 60 people from the hotel. They went right from the hotel over there to Houska Park."

"Everybody else got housed or sent to other shelters," Julie explained. I asked if there was any tracking done or how they knew where people were. Julie answered, "I would have to go through the data, but I have not done any follow-up to go back through our list. I know them all so I'll be able to go back through and say who wouldn't stay, who did, you know, that kind of thing. There was so much misinformation that it was always funny to me, Julie said. "Because, I think I've said this before, that people complained that there were 100 to 120 calls from the Econo Lodge and so they thought, *'it's a public menace, that many calls!'*"

"But I feel that, if all those people were on the streets or went into the Warming Center or something, you'd have quadrupled that number of calls out in the community, in the park, and at the Kwik Trips and Food Co-op that winter. The police reported that they really appreciated it, even the Chief did after all was said and done and all the tension between us. Even the Chief said, at the presentation we did, that the officers always had someplace they could take people. He mentioned that we always opened the doors, even in the middle of the night."

"Most of the calls were staff calling for backup so, much of the time, the police would get there and things were calmer again. There were calls where the police were called in alongside Mobile Crisis. The Chief said that most of the calls were simple problems and they weren't called for active crimes happening," Julie said, sounding pleased.

I recapped some of what Julie had shared over the afternoon at the library. We had not yet talked about the Karuna House on Grove Street in La Crosse which is the brainchild of many, including Julie, Mark, Sandy, and others, and where Julie is the Executive Director.

I witnessed an awesome story of an amazing woman in our city. To describe Julie and all she's been through, and all she's done for individuals in our City is wholly inexpressible. Thank you, Julie, so much for what you do, how you think and feel toward humanity, and for sharing your story.

Everyone is encouraged to contact Karuna House and arrange a visit or sponsor a resident, donate whatever they can, no matter how big or small, and meet Julie and her dedicated staff. It is a remarkable experience.

(The Karuna House story is told in the "Karuna House" Section earlier in the book)

Julie's Dog & Karuna Mascot, Raven

ALESHA SCHANDELMEIER

ALESHA SCHANDELMEIER is the Business and Marketing Director at Karuna House in La Crosse. She was willing to spend an afternoon to acquaint me with her work. Alesha has held other positions in the region and, most recently, as the Executive Director for several years at a nearby non-profit organization. I asked her if she welcomed the change. "One positive change related to my schedule," Alesha told me. During the years in her previous position, her work hours were more demanding including late hours, evenings, and weekends. But the raising of her three children put opposing demands on her. However, at Karuna House, her schedule holds more regular hours that enable her to be home during evenings and weekends with family. "That is really nice. It is very good," Alesha smiled. "All of my teen and young adult children live at home so it's a full house sometimes," she said. I commented, "That sounds nice to have a full house." Alesha agreed. "Yes, sometimes. Then sometimes, I feel I just might go get my own apartment!" she said jokingly.

We talked casually about the need for our own space at times, but she admitted that having her family at home is "good in most ways." She continued, "Recently, I attended a weekend community event where I was set up with my art. I had my stuff there and wasn't part of an organization or work. That was the first time I was selling my artwork with my daughter and my sister in quite some time!" Alesha said. "People were saying hi and asking me how I was doing and I'd say, *'Great!'* Then later, a couple of people said I looked so light, and I did feel lighter like I wasn't holding the weight of the world on my shoulders." It was nice to hear that Alesha's new position is benefiting her and her family.

"What do you think about working here?" I asked. "It is certainly more toned down here than my previous work. When I first started, I was just doing fill-in shifts so it was a lot of bouncing around. Then we talked about me taking over the business and marketing for Karuna House. Once the Board approved it, my job changed here. It matches the things I've done in my other positions, but I love that I get to focus on doing marketing and graphic design!" Alesha said enthusiastically. "You did just jump right in with *'The Where's Home Project'* and you did awesome work," I reminded us both.

Alesha described Karuna as a combination of energies due to the variety of people who reside there. It can be playful and youthful energy, and other times, less so. She elaborated, "It's always going to be like this, too. There may be people who leave but there will be some who never leave," Alesha said. "The population is pretty stationary. Because it's supported housing versus transitional housing, it is ideal for people to take care of their health, work, and eventually move into their own place. That would be super cool. But others won't do that and it's not a required aspect of the House. Either way, this is their home for as long as they want it. This is a safe circumstance for them and I think, probably, a lot of stress is removed to be able to live here without the pressures of change or losing their rooms."

"Sometimes a resident might get upset because we'll say, *'You need to clean up your messes.'* Sometimes it feels like dealing with children," Alesha said warmly. "But some people who have trauma histories need assistance to learn in some areas and others just didn't have the teachings when young. Some of the night staff work with residents to learn organizing and cleaning skills in their rooms."

Because Karuna House is possibly the first home in a long time and a communal living situation for many of the residents who were previously chronically homeless, I asked Alesha how housekeeping style affects the shared spaces and activities. "What are the practical aspects of the housekeeping in shared spaces, cooking, cleaning, and so on?" Alesha described a situation when a resident inadvertently threw away something that belonged to and was left out by another resident. A small conflict resulted but it allowed the residents to learn about and practice resolution, compromise, and respect for the property of others. Another resident who struggles with clutter in their room accompanied a staff member to assist an elderly person with housecleaning. It was an opportunity for the resident to learn new and improved skills. There are occasions when items are misplaced but everything at Karuna is a teaching moment.

Some of the residents knew each other and even lived closely when at Houska Park or other local encampments, according to Alesha. "I've worked with people who were housing insecure or without shelter in my previous experiences." She continued to explain that many of them were younger and in need of basic provisions, like clothing. "I'm wondering," I said, "if any of the dynamics were similar even though there is an age differential in the populations? People needing additional guidance and skill development?"

Alesha elaborated on her experience working with at-risk youth. "There were so many kids around that didn't want to identify as homeless, they were sleeping on someone's couch today, and next week, they'd be sleeping on someone else's couch. Or maybe they are staying in a car. They stay with people and their stuff is in a bag because they've been kicked out of home, you know, and it is a bad situation. So they say, *'I'm going to stay at my friend's house,'* but how long do your friend's mom and dad want you sleeping on the couch?" Alesha questioned.

I asked her, "Is there an overnight shelter for teens in our community?" "Not yet," she said and then explained there is a physical drop-in center for youth but it is not a shelter at this time. There is comfortable furniture and a place for youth to gather or rest when there is no other place for them to hang out for short periods. "Although they're working towards it," Alesha said.

Switching back to Karuna House, Alesha elaborated on the compatibility of the staff. Between the Director, Julie, and Alesha, they each cover four long-hour days that overlap during mid-week. "If I am here for too many hours, Julie is sure to let me know it is time to go home. We balance out the days that we each work without the other, so various tasks are dealt with then. Julie deals with house things on the day she's here alone, and on the day I am here alone, I deal with house things. Otherwise, we overlap with the work quite a bit the other three days. It works well," Alesha said, "It's awesome."

"I feel appreciated in this work and I really like the Board of Directors, a group of women who are sound, logical, and clear about the mission. They have a mission and it matches what the mission should be and are very dedicated to it. There are a lot of like- minded people on the Board, even though they are from many different places. This gives varied perspectives, too." I had the impression that a strong, cohesive, and varied Board of Directors enrich the Karuna experience for Alesha.

"I enjoy the residents here, too, in part because they are very different people. They all can be very reasonable and sensible when I need to reach that part of each person. Most people here can be reasoned with if we run into a problem or challenge when they are at their best."

Alesha described the multi-layered challenges the residents face. It is understood that mental health, medical, substance, and other unique issues are always present and factored in when dealing with each person. Residents may need help to do things such as remembering to take medication or get to an appointment. She explained how important it is to give positive feedback and reminders that help residents stay on task.

Residents exhibit obvious comfort living at Karuna and have accepted that this is their home. Alesha explained, "Sometimes a person might stop taking their meds and say they are fine. Now that they have a home and a room of their own, they believe that everything is good." It is still vital they continue on their medication and healthcare, Alesha conveyed, despite this misperception.

"One of the biggest challenges for me has been meeting people where they are. I think it is the hardest thing that I've had to learn since I've been here," Alesha said. "Parts of my life have been kind of toxic, as a child, and in some of adult life. It was such that we expected more of a person, as in *you just have to do better,*' you know, that sort of thing. But the realization that some people won't be doing better and don't want to move up and out, you know, gives a frustration level that I sometimes feel." I agreed with Alesha and said, "It is counter-intuitive to how most of us have been socialized to believe. Do better and rise. Do better and get out of a bad situation. Do better with an opportunity that has come your way. It is a different twist and one that makes sense when explained and understood. But still, it is intuitively the opposite of most cultural systems that reward proactive efforts and progressive advancement."

As we talked about this topic, Alesha said, "It has taken some time but, sometimes it still pops back up. I've wrestled with it because I haven't worked directly with the chronically homeless population before." I told her, "I understand your battle with this concept. I have strained my mind on this, too, and I think most people have or will. It's an important view to get right, but it doesn't come easily." She said, "I want people to do better. Once you know better you can do better and be better, but sometimes people just can't get past that point and that has to be okay, too."

To reply, I said, "In most of my interviews, I've asked if the person has a dream or goal now or from their past. Many people have said they don't, or their goal is to maintain. In my mental health career, when clients did not move forward, I accepted that coming to therapy may have been a means to maintain their life condition, rather than do better. To me, it was important to accept that, once I understood it. Substance and neurology change the level of chemicals that stir motivation and goal-setting. We aren't all the same."

"Thank God one of the residents who needs major surgery landed here," Alesha said and further explained that a pre-op procedure is crucial, too, but it can be difficult to coordinate. Alesha explained. "Most of the residents have caseworkers who coordinate this. We do help, too. We'll sit here when they make an appointment on speakerphone or support them while they make calls and set up other things like transportation."

"Often, a resident will have to activate a card that has gotten lost or become expired. We will help with this type of thing but the resident has to do the speaking while we just oversee or help to connect. It is difficult when the operator is a robot or AI, it becomes confusing for some people," Alesha explained. "But that's part of living here which, when I first started coming here, I didn't understand these limits but thought they just live here independently."

"They're supposed to do their cleaning and other things. There are a couple of staff members who help clean. But I say, *'No you don't!'* Do that, and the guys like it and know she'll clean up after them!" Alesha said with laughter although she meant what she said. "Is that frowned upon?" I asked. "That's not supposed to happen," Alesha said but explained how it is rather loosely regarded. "You know, you have to make them take care of their own stuff. Certain individuals enjoy cleaning so they end up doing quite a bit of it. I urged the others to pay that individual to do it and the tension around it would stop." And the house would be clean!"

Alesha switched topics and spoke about the differences between the two sides of the House. Karuna is a duplex-type building with resident groups on each side. "Residents buy their individual products and food. Often the food is donated and meals with leftovers are sometimes brought by. The residents look forward to this. Otherwise, it is fairly casual. "They seem to all get fed so, yeah," Alesha grinned, "But then, over on the other side though, they definitely have their stuff marked in their refrigerator."

Alesha told me about the toilet paper solution in the house. "There won't be any toilet paper usually in the bathroom because they each have their own roll and take it with them when they go. Then they take it back to their room." This is how a group of formerly unsheltered people who didn't know each other well solved the toilet paper conflict! I was impressed.

"It's just a whole different dynamic on the other side of the house," Alesha said. "They've progressed beyond some things, yeah, and they're much more independent. Just walk into one side or another and it's a completely different vibe. On one side, there might be a few more controls set in place, but they are working on each setting personal boundaries. One side may have the same type of conflict, but handle them completely different from the other side," she explained.

Alesha elaborated on community service requirements as part of the residents' living agreement. "They are to give back to the community so they can have a sense of being a part of a larger community. They seem to accept this concept in their hearts but it is difficult to follow through and complete the hours requirement, especially in the summer. There are many opportunities to work community service hours, like one-time events, attending a recovery group, helping out on a project, and so forth." Alesha described how she has posted a qualifying event on each resident's door so they are made aware of options for community service hours.

Sharing some of her personal story, Alesha explained that she was raised in northern Illinois and, eventually, her family moved outside the edge of town to live in a one- room schoolhouse. She is the oldest of four and described poverty as a family feature and chronic illness when her great-grandfather, who had neurological memory disease, lived with them.

We talked about the parallels of life in her family, former jobs, and her current job bringing rise to similar dynamics. Many people need assistance due to issues that will likely not change, which seemed to be familiar to Alesha. Being a highly functional professional, Alesha has been a leader, helper, interpreter, and peacemaker. While it may frustrate her at the early stages of learning her job, she is very good at it and has a high tolerance for being a high-functioning person amongst those who need additional and sometimes constant help.

Alesha, thank you for opening up about your new position, Karuna House, and the dynamics of the two households. You have been amazing at explaining things that can only be understood from being present there. I appreciate your generosity, creativity, and insight about the work you do and the population you assist.

JONATHAN WALTERS

JONATHAN WALTERS met with me at Karuna House to share his story. He is a staff member who works the night shift there. As a beginning point, I asked Jonathan if he was from the local area. "I am from Winona," he answered. "I moved to La Crosse when I got sober eight years ago. I just celebrated my eight-year sobriety completion on June 14th." "That's awesome!" I said. "So when you came to LaCrosse eight years ago, you were also newly sober. Would you talk about that a little?"

Jonathan continued to explain, "Yep, I had just come from jail. When I was in jail, I had an out-of-body experience." I asked him if this was the first time this had occurred. "The first time, yeah. I had died from overdoses before, four times, and once I did die. They said I had a coherent seizure. But it was actually an exorcism," Jonathan said. "I can explain it. All my muscles tensed up and I was convulsing. But I was also coherent and felt as if I was being attacked by things that I couldn't see."

"It was then that I ended up praying on my knees two weeks before, and while also in jail. I knew that there was no way for me to fix myself and I couldn't live the way that I had been. I didn't want to live the way I was and knew that drugs were going to make things worse. They already were worse than what I could handle. I was in a place where I didn't want to be. I was embracing my symptoms, seeing things, hearing things that nobody else heard or saw," Jonathan said. I asked him whether he was awake or asleep during these episodes. "It's hallucinating during the day when I was awake and then I was dreaming at night during sleep," he said. "It was a torment!"

I asked, "Were they long continuous periods? Or did they come and go, intermittently?" He answered, "It magnified that last time I was in jail a lot! But for ten years, I dealt with the same types of things. I was seeing and hearing things, and medicated. When I had seized up that day, they strapped me to a chair in the jail. They called for an ambulance and when it arrived, they strapped me into the bed inside the ambulance. I was given some sort of shot while in the ambulance."

"My body was in there but I was ascending into the air. It was all white on the sides of the road. It was just the road that had a right turn. It was just the road, the ambulance was the only vehicle on the road, and my body was in it. I was ascending and we turned right on the road. Then everything went all white. It was very vivid," Jonathan explained.

"I woke up in the hospital bed the next day and was chained to the bed. At that time, they did not put me back on any medications, no medication, but took me back to jail. I was accepted into treatment and things were different. I'd always given treatment my best effort but this was different. I knew something had happened with the clarity in my mind. I was able to function again. It was different for me, almost like I was different. It wasn't really my effort but God's effort. That's the best way I can explain it."

"I believed in things differently as if they weren't my beliefs. It was like I knew that there were answers in the Bible. I started reading the Bible when I was in treatment, and then I talked to my sponsor who had sponsored me for ten years prior. I've been through nine treatments before. So I have been through that process."

Jonathan continued by telling his story when he was younger in Winona. "I ran away when I was sixteen years old. I had a good family, a good childhood, and upbringing."

I questioned, "When you say good, what do you mean? Were you cared for? Did you know you were loved by your family?" Jonathan responded, "I wasn't abused. Our family was geared in love. We never went without anything." I asked, "So you knew you were loved by them?" He said with certainty, "Yes. And I knew that God was love. I had a good sense of what love was as well. I was never abused or anything like that."

"Can you talk about why you ran away at sixteen? What was going on?" I asked. "Because I was truant in school. As for why I ran away, I was skipping class with a friend and was put on probation. They wanted me to take a drug test and, if I failed it, and I knew I was going to fail it, they were going to send me away to treatment," Jonathan said.

"Anyway, so I ran away with a friend and we went up to the cities. I was sixteen years old and in the cities. My buddy had come with a lot of money so I was able to..." Jonathan paused. "I guess it only lasted fourteen days or, yeah, not even. The money ran out and the police came and found me there. I did go to treatment and, through that, my mom had a heart attack. It was very hard on them. They didn't know where I was so I put my parents through a lot!" I wondered, "Did your mother survive the heart attack?" "Yes. Yeah, she did." When I asked whether he was close to his parents and family, Jonathan answered, "Yeah, awesome, and my siblings, too. I have one brother and one sister." I asked, "And you're all good?" "Yep," he said. "And my parents and our family. My parents are both alive and my brother and sister are, too. What I said about a good family upbringing, our extended family and our core, my brother, sister, mom, and dad, would all get together for Christmas. For all the holidays and, for Thanksgiving we would go deer hunting with all my uncles, my dad, my brother, and my cousins. When we hunted, thirty-five guys were in our hunting party. We are close, my dad and his friends. He grew up with them and we still talk to them. So there's a huge core of just solidness in love and family upbringing," Jonathan reiterated. "Even in the friends around us and for my family time together, we don't have a split up family. I don't know any family member who we don't get along with at all, which is very hard to come by," he added. "That's just a treasure, and we don't have difficulties in our family. We just don't."

Thinking about Jonathan running away to the Twin Cities, I said, "So that's why the police found you in Minneapolis. Your parents didn't just let you go but sent the police to find you. Two weeks later, the police found you and took you back home." Answering, he said, "Yes, and I went to treatment. So from then until God changed my life when I was in jail, I had been through nine other treatments. It just had gotten progressively worse with the addiction."

To elaborate, Jonathan said, "It started with marijuana when I was twelve years old. I transferred into cocaine when I was sixteen. At about twenty-one or so I started using meth. Then when Plant Food came out, they called it Plant Food but it was Mephedrone and would be better known now as Bath Salts. *(note: Mephedrone is also known as M-cat, Meow-meow, and Plant Food. It is a stimulant related to the amphetamine family such as speed and ecstasy. It can come in powder, tablets, and capsules, and is a relatively new drug that was made illegal in 2010.)* It's kind of a different strain of uppers, but that was my drug of choice. When things really kicked into gear, I was about twenty-three and started shooting up. I wasn't just smoking anymore. I lost my girlfriend and then I ended up homeless because she kicked me out."

"I was living with somebody because I didn't have any place to live. I lost my job and wasn't even able to carry a job after I was twenty-three. So I lost everything. My parents, my mom..." Jonathan slowed and then said, "I kept asking my mom for money but she couldn't talk to me anymore because all I wanted, all I needed was money to support my habit. I would always hound her for money but she couldn't afford it. I broke her heart. She couldn't do anything to help me." I mentioned the movie, *'Basketball Diaries,'* which mirrored his decline into addiction and his mother's loving struggle to help. Jonathan shared about the movie, which he saw during recovery. "We watched that in treatment, ohh, that movie, yeah." I followed and said, "What you're talking about is that very moment your mom had to decide what to do. You describe your mom as a loving mom. Many people I've spoken with haven't had loving moms or parents."

Jonathan said, "My love for her, that's permanent. You know, I hate to say it, but even her helping me, in the understanding and looking back on it today, just feeding my addiction, it meant so much to me to get that drug. It was more than anything! I needed it to just function. I couldn't do it without the drug, so regardless of what it's for, and even in recovery now, it shows me what true love is. As you said, it's really hard to explain that because it goes against everything. For somebody who's trying to tell someone else, *'You have to get help!'* By not helping them get the drug, that's very, very hard. It's very, very difficult. I think it's even over our heads."

I responded to that by saying, "Your struggle was real, too. It's all real and such a great story that you're telling. Thank you for being vulnerable and sharing like this." "Yeah," Jonathan said. "Yeah, so I'm back to going to treatment when God changed my life. I was different and the clarity of my mind was so much different. It was such a contrast that I couldn't have even thought like that. The clarity was where I could actually think again. It was better than it had ever been before!" When I asked him how old he was during the experience, he said, "That was eight years ago. I am thirty-six years old now, so about twenty-eight." I said, "What's so awesome about this is, that many people are much older when they break through. Frequently, people have had so many years of repetition and brokenness with addiction. God decided to come to you when you were a young man."

Jonathan nodded and said, "My sponsor, like I said, had sponsored me for ten years prior. I had links with sobriety, with treatment, with hospital stays, and with overdoses. During my treatment, I was on Suboxone (*note: Suboxone is one of the main medications to treat opioid addiction.*) because I couldn't function without medication. Then they wouldn't prescribe me my medication so there were more problems on top of the addiction. The doctors would admit me into the hospital to get medication but then keep me for more than seventy-two hours which is a minimum required stay. It just turned into a terrible cycle in and out. It was terrible because I couldn't function with anything and couldn't get enough of the drugs, whether prescribed or from the street."

"It was all short-lived, so my sponsor agreed to let me live with him when I got out of treatment. It changed my life! I tried to live at my sponsor's before but he said no, because he had others who he sponsored living with him. This last time, though, was the right time for me to move in with him and he agreed with that. I lived with him for five years. He was seventy-seven years old with thirty-five years of sobriety. He chaired most of the meetings that I attended."

"Even when I wasn't able to stay sober, for years, it was ten years before I was able to stay sober, and even then, I was living with him. I rode with him to go to meetings. We would chair the meetings together and do service work. We'd close those meetings and provide for those meetings as far as cleaning the facilities, making the coffee, and just being a part of that process."

"My sponsor died three years ago, just old age, but that took a pretty good hit on me. He's not replaceable. I signed my rights over to him as he was my guardian since I lived with him. We worked that out because, mentally, I would have picked up again. He knew what would have happened, that he would have to make decisions for me. I think that's the position where I think a lot of people need to get into, where somebody is assigned to make decisions for them. When the addiction takes over or the mental health isn't strong, my sponsor was the person who told me that I could trust him. He was able to ask me, *"Do you trust me to do for you what you can't do for yourself if things change or aren't good?"* I knew mentally I couldn't put together what was right for me. I was in a good place enough to trust him and to trust myself enough to trust him. He was a Guardian Angel, and probably still is. Probably he is, yeah," Jonathan said thoughtfully.

"Were you living with him when he died," I asked. "Yes, well, I moved out when he was put into the hospital. He was moving out at that time, too, because he was ill. He had been dealing with health issues, with heart failure, and retaining water. He had water around his heart and was in ICU. He was having problems getting out of bed for a while before that and then was put in the hospital. When he had been in the ICU for a couple weeks, it happened abruptly and I knew he wasn't coming back home. If he was going anywhere, it would be somewhere with more care." I asked Jonathan where he went after that.

"I got my own place for the first time. I had gotten my own place before but it had been a disaster. I had gotten a place a couple of times. One time I roomed with somebody in recovery. They ended up slipping. It doesn't work very well to rely on somebody else's sobriety. You almost have to be with somebody who's been in recovery a long time so they can hold you accountable. You can't trust early sobriety in somebody else. My sponsor was solid enough that I knew he wasn't going to slip and he had responsibility over me, if I was going to do so."

"I could lean on him for that," Jonathan said. "He was strong enough until he got sick. The time was right for me to get my own place this time, just a trailer but I was able to manage it. It was manageable for me." Taking this moment to explain how this works, he said, "That's what it is about in recovery - manageable things. There's a lot to that because, if you can take care of something outside of yourself, it needs to be manageable. For people who are trying to help themselves, whether that's keeping a journal, if it's daily or weekly, or what makes sense to the individual like taking care of a plant, something that would flourish or that you could keep alive. Pets, possibly," he added.

"But there are a lot of unmanageable things that can ruin your life. It doesn't matter what it is. Relationships can be unmanageable for people. It's really hard if you're seeking out codependent things where you need each other to complete each other. That's a God management thing where you need to compromise for each other and let God take care of your connection. In relationships, we're trying to bring together connections. In meetings, they say that connection is the opposite of addiction. When I think about connection, I think about friction in the way that things come together. It isn't necessarily up to people. We can try on our end but God infuses things or makes them wire together."

"It doesn't matter whether it's a journal once a week, a page, or a paragraph, or a plant, a person, or a Bible verse. It is what gets you to stay where you are and move forward, not go backward. If it's a manageable thing for the person, that's a good point. The smaller, the better, the more simple, the better. That's why a lot of people have trouble with going backward because they, as people, sometimes want to take too big of a bite. Get a job, get a place, get a car, have some kids, get their kids back! So most of these are unmanageable things in recovery."

"I was a recovery coach for five years. In my first five years, after I was a year sober, I was able to get my recovery coach credentials and work as a recovery coach. That's the first thing people say right out of an overdose, *'I want my kids back!'* They don't want to change your life at all, but they want their kids back! That's why they had their kids taken away, to begin with! It's scary, you know, it is one of the biggest things when working with people – to help slow them down. You just can't start that big," Jonathan explained.

"People are pretty stubborn. They say in recovery, *'Shoot the alligator that is closest to the boat.'* That's the one that is going to get you!" he smiled. "There are a lot of things that make sense over time. Like *'Keep it simple.'* I go to these meetings regularly. I'm still involved daily with recovery meetings and with other recovery coaches as well."

"People need to address their problems and the symptoms of the problems, whether it's their upbringing, or why they do what they do, living without family. The problems can define individuals, but they don't have to. Not addressing things is not helpful. When working with people, it's good to share these things that you had to learn and battle, too. A lot of that has to do with my training, background, recovery, and coach training. What I mean is, that I may not need to experience something if I listen to someone who has had a similar experience. If we listen, we can collectively acquire a consciousness or awareness from each other. A person doesn't necessarily have to go through an experience if they listen to someone tell their own version of the experience. We can learn about it through the other person."

"That's awesome," I said, "and a way to help others before they have to go through some of the same things." "Yeah, right," Jonathan responded. Then I asked if he would share about his living situation and work.

"So after living with my sponsor for five years, I got a trailer," Jonathan began. "I was working with Coulee Collaborative at the time. That was after I had been working with Catholic Charities for two years before and also worked for the Salvation Army for a year or so. It was after those jobs, I worked with Coulee Collaborative. I was also on call at the recovery center. I was working with all the agencies that try to help people who were in the same position I had struggled with in the past."

"When I go to church, they tell me that I work in the trenches, in the snake pit, and that they could never do it. The thing is, I don't know how it works for me, but I'm qualified to do the work because I've been there."

"When society shuts people out, they don't get their health needs met sometimes. It's a sad thing when it is because of age, race, sexual identity, creed, religion, or lack of religion. They don't have a family to stick up for them, or have love around them," Jonathan said, "Nobody's going to stick up for them, not even society, and then people are ridiculed.

"When I look at something like faith, I see that we all have an individualized faith. Whether it's faith in the chair that I'm sitting in, I believe that it won't break. When you look at homeless folks, their faith is different than the majority of people. They've had to deal with everything that we haven't had to deal with - the ostracization and pushing away, and the Ways and Means, how to get what they need to survive. If we lost everything, our electricity or plumbing, we'd be trying to figure out how to live. But these people have been living without electricity for years! They already know how to do it. But we're not that far away from something happening to our comforts. We are all in the same boat in the end."

At this point, I wondered about Jonathan's home security and whether he had ever lived unsheltered, so I asked him about it. "I didn't live on the land," he answered. "I was homeless but I went from house to house, across town in Winona, couch surfing," he said. "I've gotten frostbite, walked all night while not able to get inside, but just continued to walk from one person to another. I went to trap houses for drugs because that was what I was looking for. It sounds bad but it was at least shelter."

"My shoes didn't fit me, I was frozen, and my fingertips were frostbitten. My hands and my feet were frostbitten. One winter, in particular, it was really bad. I didn't have a tent outside but I didn't live outside. My belongings were on my back, whatever I could get. I had a storage unit that I could get into for my clothes and stuff, but I couldn't live there. I would go through people's garages and try to stay in places like that, or other locations where I shouldn't be."

"I was mostly crazy and had reached a point where I wasn't able to interact with normal people anymore. Normal people, whatever that means," he said. "Segregation of the homeless, addiction, and mental health all coincide with homelessness. All these things overlap and, all of a sudden, you are your own race. You can only hang out with those people like yourself because they become your people. They understand you. And you are no longer able to talk to *normal* people. They don't understand you."

"To start a conversation, you can't even find the thought process. It had been a huge thing with me. My mental health is a thought displacement when my thoughts get all screwy. *(Note: In psychology, displacement is an unconscious defense mechanism where the mind substitutes either a new aim or object for things that, in their original form, are felt as dangerous or unacceptable.)* It's something trying to direct my path. I need to push through those thoughts and not listen to them. Sometimes they aren't what I need to be listening to. It's important to think about what you're thinking about instead of just doing what you're thinking about, and not put action to it."

"My sponsor used to say, *'You know that your head is a bad neighborhood. Don't go in there alone.'* It's sabotaging my progress. Every thought has a voice and, even before you wake up, you have a thought about the decision to wake up. *'I'm going to wake up now or I'm going to clean my room.'* Everybody thinks before they get up, before even opening their eyes. I get a lot of thoughts, too. I see negative thoughts and I know a lot of things. But they don't fester or hold. I say that because, a lot of times, I couldn't get rid of certain thoughts. It's what they call the schizophrenia in my life."

"But my recovery coach got a kick out of this. They called it The Dirty Bird. *'If you let The Dirty Bird fly through your mind, you shouldn't let it nest, because it will have babies. If you sit there and think about it, all of a sudden, they're gonna hatch out and have more babies and be a bunch of Dirty Birds. So if you see The Dirty Bird, let it fly through, just let it fly through. Let it go and don't let it nest. Don't hang on to it,'* he would tell me."

"What I found, if that thought stops and I can't get rid of it, I offer it to God as a sacrifice. I like to say, too, that it's living because it's living to me. So I give it as a living sacrifice to God and then it's gone,"

Jonathan said with conviction. I told him, "It's been a privilege to hear your story. Would you share where you are now, with home and work? Are you still in your trailer? You seem quite happy now. I think you've come a long way."

Jonathan talked about his living situation and the work he does. "From my trailer, I bought a house two years ago. I sold the trailer and bought a house. Now I'm paying off my house. It is a nice house that I never thought I would ever own. I never thought that a house was possible for me. I was in debt for jail, from jail stays. I was in debt from the fines I owed to the court. So just a lot of being in the hole. I don't have my mortgage paid off yet but I am paying it off. I'm making my payments. I'm able and it's manageable for me to pay my mortgage off. I'm working in that direction."

"From the streets to your sponsors, then to your trailer, and now to your house. You have made wonderful progress," I told Jonathan. He said, "Yeah, eight years of sobriety and two years of the house." I replied, "So eight years ago, if someone said this is where you'd be right now, what would you have said?" Jonathan said, "Well, it's a mansion where I live. I mean compared, I couldn't think that I would ever be capable of this in my life. I treat it as beyond my dreams. It feels like who I am and, yeah, it says in the Bible that our house is our body, or about how he's given us this temple. Where I live and keep my house clean, they say this in recovery, and it's important to me as well, that as far as my body goes, I work out and take care of myself physically. It helps me mentally very much and spiritually. I can't control anything else, that's what it's about. It's either having control or power or seeking some sort of control or power."

"There's strength in numbers, even in recovery. If there are ten people for a meeting, they say that's a power greater than yourself. By yourself, you can't do as much as you can with ten people. What is more powerful and what you'll eventually reach is God. For me, where I am in my life and what I look at, is the way God has changed me."

Jonathan speaks about his gratitude. "My family, I'm very fortunate for my family. For what God has done in my life, for my belief, for who I am. We all get that knock on the door but we don't answer. As for my family, my mom is happy. My aunt, my uncle, godparents, are all very close to me. My other aunt and uncle as well. When I drive through town and go by where they live, each one, I stop at their house. My aunt brought me some flowers that she dug out of her garden for me to plant. I have gotten to taking care of stuff outside of myself again."

Describing some of what he cares for, Jonathan said, "I got my little ducklings that I hatched out. I got a double pond in my backyard for them. They hatched out their little ones and got babies. They're not The Dirty Birds! They're the fun ones! I have a couple of chickens and just the beautiful stuff, a beautiful view of the back, and my pond overlooks what I have."

"What's next for you?" I asked him. "What dreams or goals do you have?" "It's interesting you ask that," Jonathan said, "Because I think I'll just pay off what I have and take care of what I have. I've been studying God's dwelling and I want to be where God is at all times. That is my dream. I want to help people in the capacity that God can help people and that's what I want for myself. I want to be able to give them what they want for themselves. I think there's excellent value in that. As far as my purpose to others and what I want for myself, you can't work with people unless you're willing to work with them where they are. We want to give them what they need rather than what they want. But they're able to excel if we can help to give them what they want and see where they're able to go from there."

"What did you want that was your answer eight years or before?" I asked. "What would you have said if someone said to you, *'What do you want, Jonathan?'* He answered, "Well, that's interesting you say that because I didn't want. I just wanted money for drugs. But I wanted to clear my head and then God came in. My mind got so screwed up that I wanted God to come in and clear it, take me the way I was. I told him that and I was on my knees. I just knew there wasn't anything that anybody or I could do to help me anymore. I didn't want to be the way I was anymore."

"Like I said about the experience, just share it. If you just share your experience, that is the best way to address somebody else's life. Work with people where they're at and work with what they want. If there's even a sliver of what they want, work with the sliver. They're going to keep moving. They're going to keep going. That's just human nature."

Thank you, Jonathan, for your amazing recovery story. You are a true role model and man of faith. I appreciate the community work you do by helping others and keeping the parks of La Crosse clean and safe through your Parks & Rec work.

BARB POLLACK

BARB POLLACK spoke with me in the office at Karuna House where she is a staff member. To confirm with Barb, I asked, "You have not been homeless but you've experienced home insecurity, is that correct?" She said, "I'd say close to it."

Barb continued to tell her story. I stayed in this area my whole life, had three children, and was divorced. So I raised my three kids as a single mom in La Crosse and Onalaska." I asked about her work and she explained that she raised her children without a college degree. "Fast forward to where I am now. I can even go back when I was married." She hesitated and then said, "A lot of people don't know this, but I'm not ashamed about it because it's a part that makes me relatable to other people."

"I don't have an addiction. I don't, thank God. But I went to prison for a year and a lot of people who know me do not believe that I was incarcerated." Barb continued frankly with her story. "I was in a bad situation in my marriage," she said and continued to unroll the details of her circumstances that led to her spending a year imprisoned.

Being incarcerated brought a combination of positive and negative aspects together for Barb. Because it was almost twenty-five years ago, her children were young and in elementary and high school. This made her sentence even more difficult to shoulder. She was away from family with little contact, but the confinement helped her to deepen her faith, strengthen her voice, and broaden her life experiences with different people and varied activities.

Barb explained one aspect that was a true blessing. "I didn't realize that God was walking along with me. But where it got really cool was the blessing that came out of it. God puts every bad thing that happens to us and turns it into good! My parents stepped up and said *'We'll take the kids.'* They still got to see their dad and my parents got to be with my kids! They were able to bond and make such a special relationship with my parents."

Barb continued, "My parents had a purpose again and my kids learned so many great things from them. Their school was so great. They knew I was gone so they helped out in every way that they could. Up to the present, my dad still has a great relationship with all my children. He is eighty-eight years old. My mother passed away four years ago.

Another blessing, it was just eye-opening. I didn't know God was opening up the doors for me while I was away. For my job at the prison, I got to work at the daycare. On the weekends, I went to another building where the parents could be with their kids. When I came back home, my life was different," Barb said. "I was much stronger. It was just really freeing for me," she explained.

Eventually, Barb became a single parent and worked at a golf course for ten years. She and her children lived in her childhood home. "It could have been so much different," she explained. "My kids would have gone to foster care. I could have lost my kids! I could have turned to addiction. I could have done all these things but, no, because of the grace of God, my kids didn't have to go to foster care. They didn't have to have a life where a dysfunctional cycle could have started," Barb said with relief. "I love my family."

Elaborating about her family situation, Barb said she did not make a lot of money, but she didn't have to worry about supporting her family because she was safe and secure in her family's home. Speaking about her children, she said, "They were in a good school district, too." She continued, "One day I was taking my daughter to an appointment and I looked in a magazine that said, *'Do you want to go back to school?'* It was a program called the Self-Sufficiency Program."

"Oh my goodness," she said, "It was a free program. So, I called and it was a week before it was going to start that spring. A lady named Amy Sullivan said, *'Get your application in!'* and I was accepted! I started going to this program once a week and didn't have to secure daycare because it offered free daycare if you wanted. At that time, it was held at Viterbo University, but it was through the University of Wisconsin La Crosse (UWL).

"I learned how to write papers, how to balance my life, and have stability in my school. It was just amazing. I was with other women and men who wanted to go back to college. When I was done, I discovered that I could go to college." Barb explained that she lacked confidence in her abilities, but she went right into the University of Wisconsin and was accepted. "Here I am, a single parent with three kids, divorced and working full time at a golf course. But I got a chance to go to the University when I never thought I would!"

Barb questioned, "What was I going to do? Psychology? I wanted to help people, right? I didn't know what made me think of that, so I just started taking classes and working. All of a sudden, doors started opening up for me! I took a women's gender studies class and fell in love with the professors. I started taking the women and violence class which intrigued me." Time passed while she continued her studies and Barb was "kicked out of school," she said with a smile, "because I had too many credits after taking so many classes! They told me, *'Barb, you have to graduate one of these days!'*"

"I was there for six years and was a Super, Super Senior! I graduated in 2015 but, you know, my gosh, I loved the Self-Sufficiency Program *(SSP)* so much that I thought, *'I have to be a part of that!'* Now I'm on the board of SSP and I help teach it. It's at UWL and still going today every fall and spring. I still help out because it's so important. I am grateful to Andrea Hansen and Jan for keeping the program strong. Students who go to that class get scholarships for four semesters in addition to free food."

"Doors continued to open for me so I kept walking. All of a sudden, I worked for La Crosse County for four years. I was in Mobile Crisis Responder for mental health and addiction. I also left the golf course and worked at Gunderson in dietary. Every year while I was in the Gundersen Health System, I wanted to do something different. I couldn't believe how my confidence was building. A year later, I went to another department, and another year later, to another department. Pretty soon, I was on Great Rivers 211 answering crisis phone calls."

As Barb continued to explain her journey through work, she said, "I met Julie after I graduated from UWL. They were looking for a collaborative team for homelessness. They hired Julie and were looking for some outreach personnel. I said to myself, *'You know what I think? I need to do that!'* So then, I just went out in the streets. I mean, every door has been opened for me so far, why stop now? So I did that and thought, *'You know, I'm working with over a hundred people out there. I want to make a difference and work more closely with the people!'* So, I applied for CouleeCap to do case management and worked very closely with people in supportive housing. I became a supervisor and worked there for about five years."

"I just changed jobs again and am now working at St. Clare Health Mission and have been there for over a year," Barb said. She described some of the work she does which includes supervising the Community Health Workers. "I just look back at my life," she said, "and think of how I could have been on the edge." I replied, "You sure could have, but you didn't go over." "I didn't go over," Barb answered softly, "because I had the support of other people."

"I've seen my best friend die of alcoholism. I've seen so many people who I've met die out in the street. I've used Narcan on people and I've seen it all," she said. "But I'm here." We talked for a few minutes about all she had been through and how her life had evolved positively. Then Barb said, "When people talk about going away, they say, *'I can't go to treatment, I can't do that!'* I say, *'Yeah, you can!'* and then I say, *'I've been away from my kids for a whole year! I know what pain is!'* They don't believe me when I tell them this."

After hearing Barb's amazing story thus far, I asked her if she had siblings. "I do have two older brothers, yes." She explained that they are close and "the entire family is super close. My brothers were the straight-A students. I was, you know, well, there is always an odd-one-out in the family but they were always there. My parents would say, *'Why didn't you tell us you were going through that? We would have paid or helped!'* but that wasn't the point. The point was, I did it." Barb explained about taking responsibility and being imperfect. "God doesn't want the perfect people, right? He didn't pick his disciples from the perfect people. He picked the people who were broken and dysfunctional. That's who he wants."

Barb opened up about her journey as a Christian, from childhood and how it grew over the years. Then she said, "I'm a Christian. I believe the Bible. There's a guy who said, *'He never answers my prayers.'* And this is what I say to them all the time, *'He answers in three different ways. He either says yes, no, or maybe, not right now.'* I always give an example that helps explain this. I absolutely trust God with everything, so that's what gets me through all the hard times."

Barb described her Gratitude Book in which she writes down good and bad things that happen. "I even write the bad things I am grateful for because I know there's going to be something good and grateful in it. There's good in everything. God promises that."

"The only time I've ever wanted to think to myself, *'I cannot go on,'* the one time I've ever been the lowest in my life was right after I found out about my legal situation. I remember laying in my bathtub, feeling alone, but now I know today that I was not alone that day. God was with me.

"I love being here," she said. "I like being around these guys. I love it. This is part-time, super part-time. I work all day on Mondays at my other job, and then come over here right after to just hang out with the Karuna residents. I was just working with the other tenant trying to help her out with some things. I only work until eight," she said. "I'm old and have to be in bed by 8:30!" she laughed. "Sometimes I'll do a weekend day if somebody needs a day off."

To close our conversation, I asked Barb about her children who are grown now. "I'm a grandma for the first time! Three months!" she said as she pointed to a picture on the door. "That is my granddaughter on the door! She's the love of my life! My oldest son is 37 and he's doing great. They've been married a couple of years and that's their baby, Georgia. Then my daughter, Katy, who is 32 years old. My youngest, Scotty, is 29 and not married. He is a busy guy who works for the school district and also coaches baseball in Onalaska. He loves all sports. All three of my children are doing pretty good," Barb said with a smile.

My gratitude to Barb for sharing her struggles and blessings as she finds her way through what could have been a much worse outcome. Thanks for sharing about your family, faith, and positive outlook. You are a true role model!

WHERE'S HOME?

MARK SCHIMPF

MARK SCHIMPF sat with me at Jules for coffee one morning to share his story. "I work in healthcare," he began without hesitation. "I was last a community health worker for a partnership between Gundersen Health System, now Emplify, and St. Clare Health Mission, a free clinic in town that serves people who have no insurance."

"A community health worker is meant to be like a bridge maker. There's a lot of bridges to be built between healthcare and people who are homeless," Mark explained. "Perhaps one of the contributing problems to homelessness is health issues. Homelessness is a huge factor in their disconnection from the healthcare system, accessing them, and helping to support their health. It also is a challenging influence when attempting to sustain what help is put in place."

"Some of the sickest people are in our homeless community. When I say *'sick'* I mean physically sick with chronic, challenging illnesses like later-stage diabetes, COPD, and cancer. They're out there! All this to say, there are a lot of healthcare gaps."

"My work was to see people in the emergency room who either identified as homeless through the hospital records, or they self-identified as such, or the staff just had kind of an inkling there were some unmet social needs. I attempted a kind of outreach by sitting and talking with them. If there were people I knew who were an access point and were willing to sit in the ER, Gundersen is interested in this sort of thing."

"Individuals who are homeless come into the ER appearing as though they're not accessing primary care. They either come in on their own, just walk in, are brought in by people, or just end up there from psychiatric emergencies which become exacerbations of their chronic illnesses. They just ended up there, so my work was to try to help them by offering primary care."

"I also had the chance, in that role, to go out with the street medicine team. They did a big fundraising effort with Rotary and now have a mobile clinic that has two full rooms," Mark explained enthusiastically. "It's a full clinic. They can choose separate private rooms, heated or cooled. It's a mobile health clinic and really interesting work. It goes out generally on Wednesday mornings, I recall. During my time, we'd scout down by the river and the encampments where there were a lot of people, or go by the Warming Center or Salvation Army, and park the clinic. People just came. I would also go out and do some groundwork beforehand. People reminded other people that we would be there in the morning."

"If I knew that something was especially going on, I'd say, *'Hey, how about we try and talk to the doctors tomorrow and see what they can do to help you?'* If they just seemed particularly sick, I'd try to prod them toward that."

"The street medicine team is comprised of a supervising doctor and family medicine residents who come along for the experience. There was a nurse, usually Sandy Brekke, and I drove and did follow-up work. Some people have big things that need care, so we'd schedule them for follow-up at the clinic. I did do the legwork to help people follow through with their appointments."

Mark continued, "I think this model helped build trust between part of mainstream society and really disenfranchised people. It humanized some elements of being doctors in this case and building solid relationships with those doctors and the medical team. The doctors were able to come out of their offices and see this kind of service."

Elaborating on his career path, Mark explained, "I trained and worked as an EMT, and then went into nursing school. I started as an EMT in 2023 after leaving Saint Clare Health Mission in January 2020. I wanted to progress into that work to be doing something more mainstream in healthcare. I still had some time to wait before my nursing classes began. So I worked as an EMT before it started last fall. I'll be done this December!" Mark said.

"The medical outreach experience with the street medicine team led me to this. Even though I was the Gopher," Mark smiled, "I saw a lot of really good work which influenced my track. It was good and interesting work with people who don't access medical care and don't even dream of it."

"It's not what we're known to do in our culture," I added. "These last several generations are all about preventative care, vaccinating, dental and eye checkups." Mark said, "This population just does not because they have some distrust in the medical system. I'm not saying that it's their fault because, I think, there are very valid reasons. That trust gets broken or they don't feel heard. They don't get their full treatment or something happens to them. They see this part of the issue and they're not wrong about that, no, especially if they have substance use currently or in their background. The medical system and providers immediately see that and treat them differently. *Immediately.*" Mark emphasized.

"There's a lot of unconscious bias," Mark explains, "I think this manifests in slightly different care. People come in for substance use and sometimes have challenging behaviors, or any number of other things. They've got a lot going on in their lives that we're going to see especially in the ER. For those two hours, we have snapshots and, sometimes, that snapshot is quite negative."

"I think it causes a lot of people in healthcare to think that a patient like this is drug seeking or pursuing attention. Many reasons cause their medical legitimacy to be doubted. They don't have credibility as a patient. I don't necessarily fault the medical professional individually. It's a systemic, capital H healthcare problem rather."

"It's a moral devaluate that allows a tolerance of this kind of injustice. There is a kind of moral repugnance of homelessness which is not morally permissible under any system. It is inherently immoral," Mark stated. "People are worth something, but the continued existence of homelessness, as it stands in this country, relies on us devaluing people."

"I think we need to have a clear stance of a worthiness calculi. I used to think a lot about worthiness and, I guess, that's like a fill-in for moral standing. We decide, even within homelessness, that some people are, yes, the good homeless. That there's a model of homelessness."

"It's unfathomable until you experience homelessness. It's a privilege to not experience it. We have privilege so we don't think it's that, not until we lose it. We have the privilege of not seeing how important our homes are. That's intense! And then if you lose that, you're just living in survival mode."

"My experience with people living outside is they're not thinking about even day-to-day, but it's hour-to-hour. *What am I going to do in the next hour? Where am I going to find food? How am I going to keep my stuff? Where am I going to get my drugs?'* It's always right there in the present. They are stuck, absolutely stuck, right there. No privacy, no security, nothing. That isn't a foundation from which positive change arises. Some people probably do it and have done it, for sure. But it comes back to connection, I think," Mark concluded. "That's why something like Karuna House works so well,"

"It's an intentional community and residents decide to be a part of it. They are offered a spot obviously, or however Julie and the organization are doing that, but it's an intentional community. The individual decides to show up to that environment. That aspect is very significant. It's the keystone of the model and it's no coincidence. Once you have that connection, security, and dignity back, maybe drugs aren't..." Mark paused.

"I hear what you're saying," I said. "Like you being on the mobile medical team and having that association. You absorbed that experience which enabled the next possibility. It is what sent you to the next point in your life, which you may or may not have gotten to otherwise. On our trajectory, we say *'I want to be this. I want to do that. I want to be a nurse.'* People living homeless who I have interviewed are perplexed when I ask if they have had hopes or ideas about their aging or later-life housing, or their near future. I've asked about past dreams or goals, too, but it is rare to hear someone who had an idea or plan about progression or a trajectory of some kind. There is definitely a loss of hope and selfhood, of creative thought, and a world from which they are disenfranchised."

Mark responded, "The loss of that connection is kind of the loss of connection to a part of yourself, to the mainstream community. Hour-to-hour survival and chronically in survival mode, especially if the weather is bad, has its ways that cause people to get involved in very challenging things."

"It's not, *'One week I was housed in the middle class and today I am homeless.'* No, it is not how it goes!" Mark described. "Nobody becomes homeless in one day. I would have to work toward that end." Mark explained that, at some point in life, we have built-in supports such as spouses, supportive families, and homes. "People have to get pretty far in the margins to actually become suddenly homeless," he said.

"There are a lot of people who appear to live well but are on the margins but may never fall over," I interjected. "Nobody ever really knows about their neighbors and how close to the edge they may be, especially in the senior population. I purchased my home in La Crosse from the family of an elderly woman who was still working her long-term job when she committed suicide in the garage. She was in her seventies and terrified of her financial vulnerabilities, and possibly losing her home and safety. She had extended family and grown children."

"In warmer climates, the senior population is the rising number of homeless living in cars and vans. Many women over seventy are living in desert homeless encampments. On the other end of life, it's health, insurance, and social security issues that are all stakes and push people to the margins. Through my interview experiences, I've heard stories about how *'everything was good! We had a house, paid our mortgage, and then...I was homeless.'* It's likely a slower process than that, but it's not always slow enough!" I suggested.

Mark said, "It's like a culmination, I think. I'm not going to discount that some people abruptly become homeless. But I think there has to be more because of how it relies on marginalization. I think people who have the privilege to not think about it or even comprehend it because they're not that close to it."

"Given everything we know about how it's generational, it often sets you on that road before you have the opportunity to start making choices for yourself. At least some of the people who I've worked with in the past, have never known privacy, security, or help from someone. They've never relied on anyone. They've done all sorts of things to cope with, just basically, not to die. That's all they've ever known in one way or another."

Continuing, Mark said, "There was a retired doctor at the Warming Center when I worked for Catholic Charities. I checked after he said that he was a retired doctor because it sounded unreal to me. It just sounded too much or too big. But I found out that it was true. He has since passed away but was housed, I believe, when he died. He was one of our oldest at seventy-five-years-old in the shelter," Mark described.

"How long does someone bounce between the zone before becoming homeless and living outside?" Mark questioned. "You might spend a little bit of time in shelters, on people's couches, then after doing that for two or three years, everything kind of falls in, having no friends left to stay with, no favors left to claim," Mark explained.

I added, "This doctor who was homeless, he might have lived a life where he had money, and a home, but how it was all put together may have been more shaky." Mark confirmed, "It's not like, one day, he was a doctor making all sorts of money. He made some questionable choices as a doctor, by his admission, based on what he felt comfortable telling about his story. The rest is hearsay but still interesting.

His whole life was pretty turbulent, in his professional practice, it was challenging. But, even he had to take a long time to end up just flat out on the street."

"But again, it's that distance, the fact that marginalization is such a big factor. 'Normal' people can't even comprehend the system and how it happens. That makes it easy to think, *'They deserve it. They probably did something wrong.'* We blame them because homelessness is seen as morally repugnant," Mark stated.

"I think the mental health part of it is probably a key, even beyond the family structure. Even if there was a good family structure, as young people start to develop the symptoms over ten years or so, they start to do drugs and become addicted. The original mental health circumstances they were born with are something that the general public doesn't think about," Mark points out.

"We've spent a lot of time wringing our hands about how to help people in this population. *'How do we do it? How do we affect any sort of change?'* The discussions between Julie and I are moral philosophy conversations about homelessness," Mark smiled, and then he continued, "and, ultimately, people must be housed for a real and lasting change to be the expectation. It's Maslow's. You have to have physical safety taken care of before working on the other stuff," Mark said. *(Note: Maslow's Hierarchy of Needs is a theory in psychology that places human needs on a five-level pyramid. The lower-level needs that include food, water, safety, and shelter must be met before ascending to higher needs that include a person's psychological, belonging, or self-esteem needs.)* People who have never had a problem with physical needs from birth, don't understand this hierarchy of needs."

"It starts from birth, being healthy, and making good choices. But we need to have our physical needs fulfilled before we can begin working on self-attainment. For people in the community or our neighbors, the chief tasks are to see the challenging behavior in the homeless community and mislabel it as liking to party, having a good time, and living outside as if it's summer camp."

"But none of them are having fun or enjoying themselves!" Mark firmly states. "It's not of their choosing. I think, to most people deep down if they think about it, homelessness doesn't sit right with them," Mark said thoughtfully. I responded by saying, "They might just be too afraid. I mean, the obvious end, if we stop making our efforts to stay where we are or to progress, whether by choice or by circumstances, is the loss of home and everything affiliated with it. This is what keeps us going - the belief and hope that we are doing it right, and they did it wrong," I said.

Mark added, "It is a vivid and very graphic reminder to think that they are us. It's like you, too, could be chewed and spit out, thrown out, and harassed by the police. We use that choice thing. If it's that they're choosing it, choosing to use drugs then this is what happens."

I then said, "But it's in all the stories and films historically. Average people are portrayed as doing well, but then lose everything, from home to credibility and value. It can be from our choices, disease, domestic violence, accident, war, or just anything. People are deep-down very afraid of what will become of them."

Making a shift to Mark's personal history, I asked him, "Do you know of a time in your life when you either didn't know about the things we're discussing or didn't feel them as you do now? What may have changed for you as you grew older and matured?"

After giving it some thought, Mark began, "I grew up in eastern Wisconsin in the Fox Valley. I didn't know what homelessness was but I remember going to Madison when I was a kid. My first big brush with it was on State Street. To this day, a large homeless thing happens there at times. I remember that being really confusing to me."

"I was in middle school at the time and I remember puzzling over it, *'Why did they live out here?'* My instructions from adults in my life were, *'Don't talk to them. Don't give them money. Don't do anything!'* Okay, yeah, but why are they asking for money? It was confusing," Mark disclosed.

"I don't remember my parents' explanations well enough, but I remember that it impacted me. I recall thinking, *'Wow! There are so many people!'* It was winter and people were hobbled up in the door-ways. They were sleeping outside. It was cold, just freezing out. I couldn't feel my hands while walking around. I remember this bothering me and having this sentiment about it. I felt something stronger but I didn't know what to do with that."

"Then I went off to school. I went north to Northland College in Ashland, Wisconsin where there isn't a lot of visible homeless, mostly because it is so hard to live outside up there. They'd get burned in the summer and frozen over in the winter!" Mark said strongly. "It's just inhospitable!"

"I worked at a Burger King during college. I never knew where he lived exactly but, a man came in regularly and occupied a seat. Especially in the winter when I worked there, he just kept buying cups of coffee. He'd lose Styrofoam that he wouldn't see as it crumbled to the floor, which I remember because I was the one who did the cleaning up! The man always carried around a bunch of Styrofoam, which I now realize he may have used for insulation that crumbled off."

"He was an interesting fellow, clearly had some serious mental health problems as he sat there talking to himself. He hit that archetype, writing in a notebook full of scribbling. He wasn't a young person but he was clearly able to carry all his belongings. At the restaurant, we just tolerated him because he was buying something and never really caused any trouble."

"I have thought about him a lot, too. I can still see his face. He just came in for his coffee and kept getting it. Maybe, at the time, it was a dollar? I don't think any fast food restaurant does that anymore, precisely because people would use it as a way to stay warm," Mark said.

"These are things I have thought about but not super actively. I didn't really make any sense of it and it still doesn't, to be honest. I don't really understand it and it's hard for me to wrap my head around it."

"I went to grad school in Idaho. That's another story, but nothing there, just living in northern Idaho for two and a half years. Then I came to La Crosse because my now-wife, then-girlfriend got into graduate school at UWL. So I just moved here sight unseen," he said. I told him, "You picked two of the coldest places in the northern U.S. for your advanced education where there probably wasn't a lot of homelessness." "Yes," Mark said. "But

La Crosse was the first time I saw a permanent population of homeless in a city."

"I was twenty-four and, at that point, I knew that there was a warming center at the Baptist Church on West Avenue where people were stacked up outside waiting. It was before the current warming center," he said.

"There was a cold snap that lasted about three weeks and, I remember, that the Wesleyan Methodist Church on King Street was the designated emergency shelter. That was at least ten years ago. But I volunteered there after I saw the appeal go out for volunteers. It was interesting to sit around and talk to people and hear what people had to say. There was a woman there who had birds that she carried around with her for some reason. I think she had been recently homeless at the time. That was my first time meeting some of the people who, at that point, I was meeting for the first time but would come to know extremely well."

"That has stuck with me," Mark said. "So far, all these described events from your life stuck with you, even as a boy," I remarked. "Yeah," Mark said and then, "I worked at a hotel for a year, when I first moved here. I was also in AmeriCorps as a volunteer. It is a federal volunteer program. I worked with CouleeCap and the City of Lacrosse Planning Department. This was a format that held forty different meetings around town, some of them with the public, some of them just with directors and boards. This was an attempt to understand what our community sees as gaps in the City's needs. Homelessness just shot through everything, at that point. It was unifying," Mark said. "It was a big step when I met a lot of people, including Julie, I think, but I'm not sure exactly if this is where I met her."

"I remember we were able to learn what people thought, and who had the resources to do what they needed, even if they weren't necessarily homeless. This helped me get to know the community quite a bit."

Mark shifted to talk about his work with shelters in La Crosse. "In most shelters, people are asked to choose, *'Do you want safety or do you want autonomy? Do you want security or do you want dignity?'* I think solutions that ask you to trade one necessary human thing, something that is absolutely fundamental to being a human, for another is not a solution. It's coercion," Mark stated. I added, "It's like saying something so base as *'Do you want to breathe or do you want to see?'*" Mark responded, "Correct, you are right. It's absolutely, you must choose between two things that we would never negotiate and that, to us, are so innate. To us, it would be, *'What do you mean, I've got to choose whether I can keep my cherished albeit very large suitcase of belongings or I can sleep inside!'*"

Mark said, "Fundamentally, in shelters for pragmatic reasons, it is understandable because we're trying to run this thing and not have it close. They're not funded well and because you can't be a circus. Shelters need organization and control. I think shelters are put in impossible positions," Mark pondered. "It would be great if shelters could offer privacy, warmth, comfort, security, nutrition, and everything else. But in reality, we're always asking somebody to make a trade-off."

"As it is," he said, "those in homelessness are offered a case worker who advocates for them. They convince a landlord to give them a unit. But it's a trade-off. Already the landlord is going to surveil the tenant. They can't even have visitors or invite their homeless friends to come around. Nobody can stay because the landlord is going to be watching. So they just traded off their privacy, their connection to the community, and their freedom to associate with others for shelter."
"The tenant is then evicted and we shuffle another person in. That's the hope, that it falls apart and the public doesn't have to think of a solution. There's a lot of vulnerability when a person shows a desire. Will they achieve it? Is it correct? Are they going in the right direction? It's a big step," Mark said. "Trying to foster positive change is a big risk for the person making it."

"To be placed at such risk just to be allowed housing is not a gain, but a loss of self-esteem, person-hood, and a home. Living outside is not the norm, but it's a bunch of people in survival doing whatever they can. It's survival!" Mark said with emotion. I responded, "Humans have never chosen to live outside. Even from the very beginning, Cavemen lived inside. In caves! Nomads wandered but developed villages when they built huts and began irrigating crops. The only reason people moved around was to follow the food and provisions, hunting and gathering. But as we civilized, we chose to stay put, inside shelters." Mark responded, "That's good. As it turns out, we need that sense of place."

I said, "People want to identify with their group or a group. Our town is our 'hometown.' But we bull-doze the encampments as if they are meaningless and not anyone's homes, albeit temporary." Mark said, "We can't force people to change. We're not responsible for that change. But we need to support it and be alongside them. Hopefully that change comes from within them," he said. "hopefully we can foster it. That's the big thing in homelessness, that sometimes we take a little too much credit for people." I said, "Yes, I see what you mean. If it works, we did it. If it fails, they did it." Mark replied, "We need to work alongside and empower and cultivate, and just hope they respond to that and that they will want the change. If the conditions are right, we can work with them and help them," he concluded.

"Mark, you have done a lot so far in your career and helped many people. You have shared a lot here today about that work and the people you've met. I've learned about your experiences and thoughts regarding this community, in La Crosse and the homeless situation. What is next for you?"

"People have died while they were homeless. They have died because homelessness is a terminal chronic illness," Mark poignantly stated. "I like Hospice," he said. "I like that work at least so far. We're doing it now," he said. "I'm an intern," Mark said, seemingly happy about it.

"What appeals to me is that it's, again, not telling people how things should be or how they should do things. I can just provide a supportive situation, with no judgment, and offer them their options." I reflected, "That's like working with the homeless just as you have described. Offering options, not making them choose or make a compromise between their needs." Mark answered, "Yes, I'm bringing that into a different situation, right? I'm taking some of the ethical ideas I've picked up working in homelessness and, what homelessness has taught me. Working with people who are homeless has taught me so much and I'm trying to apply that to a totally different cycle of life."

Mark, congratulations on your new career direction. It is a wonderful segue for your life's work. Thank you for sharing your depth of experience and insight for 'The Where's Home Project' and the 'Where's Home' book. I very much appreciated the time and knowledge you committed to this interview. Thank you.

ACKNOWLEDGMENTS

Acknowledgments

Special appreciation for these people who will always be remembered for their contribution to this book and *The Where's Home Project.* Some are organizers, planners, donors, and workers of all kinds, and many are warriors!

***The Where's Home Project* Collaborators:** Sister Karen Neuser FSPA, Hannah Amann, Bobbi Rathert, Eileen Gray, Julie McDermid, Alesha Schandelmeier, Rachel McFarland, Roxanne Aubrey, Emily Boland, Sister Karen Kappell FSPA

Interviewees: Trish Lisota, Joey Abey, Michael Engrebretson, Trinj, Jana Boland-Windbiel, Ryan Marks, Heather Archer, Greg, Lucas DeLorenzo, Barb Pollack, Brad and Zen, Jonathan Walters, Marcos Perez, Mark Schimpf, Jeffrey Brandt, Bubba , June Hart, Julie McDermid, Alesha Schandelmeier